After the loss of her son, J.J. followed her thirst for information on the afterlife (Heaven), reincarnation and past lives. She received Reiki (hands-on energy healing) treatments and subsequently became a Reiki Master /teacher so she could treat others. J.J. also practiced angel card therapy daily for herself and others if they were interested.

While visiting four psychic mediums and a tarot card reader, J.J. "spoke" to her son receiving amazingly accurate information from him and other spirits that helped her with her healing. She will share this inspiring information with you.

J.J. details the first three years after Ryan's passing and hopes that relaying her trials and suggestions for dealing with them will assist YOU on your healing journey too.

Ryan's Legacy

How To Survive the Loss
of Your Loved One

To my very good friend,
Light and love,
JJ Southwell

J.J. SOUTHWELL

BALBOA.
PRESS

A DIVISION OF HAY HOUSE

Balboa Press books may be ordered through booksellers or by contacting:

Balboa Press
A Division of Hay House
1663 Liberty Drive
Bloomington, IN 47403
www.balboapress.com
1-(877) 407-4847

ISBN: 978-1-4525-7385-4 (sc)
ISBN: 978-1-4525-7387-8 (hc)
ISBN: 978-1-4525-7386-1 (e)

Library of Congress Control Number: 2013908145

Printed in the United States of America.

Balboa Press rev. date: 05/15/2013

To our beloved son and brother, Ryan
Jan. 9, 1978-Nov. 39, 2009

Contents

Part One

Ryan chose this picture to be his profile picture on Facebook. In that way, he chose the picture that I used to frame and place on his casket at his wake. Now it sits on a table beside my chair and I see it first thing in the morning and the last thing at night.

I can't believe it.
Ryan has died.
He lost his battle with cancer.
He was only thirty one years old.
Why did God take him so young?
I wish I were dead too.

Ryan's Story

Ryan had just finished university and came out with a degree in computer software engineering. He got a brand new apartment in a recently erected building near center town in Ottawa, Ontario. He started his own company and did contract work for other larger companies. This was a great start to his new career.

Then, I got the phone call. He told me that he had a sore on his tongue and it didn't seem to want to heal. I suggested that he should go to our family dentist to see if he could shed some light on the situation. Our dentist sent him to a specialist who was a friend of his.

Another call told me that he had cancer on his tongue also known as oral cancer. Well, you could have scraped me off the sidewalk with that news. I had a hole in my chest the size of a basketball. This wasn't really happening to Ryan, my son. This was not really happening to me; but it was!

I kept wondering, "Why would God do this to Ryan? Why would God do this to me? What did we do wrong? Why was He punishing Ryan? Why was He punishing me? Why do we always blame God at times like this?

Within a few months, Ryan had surgery on his tongue. They took out a pie-shaped piece from his tongue. One of the side effects could have been a problem with his speech. But remarkably, Ryan's speech was almost normal with only a slight lisp, and only occasionally. Eventually he was given a clean bill of health. We were elated to say the least. He continued to have regular check-up appointments with his doctors and everything seemed to be going very smoothly again. His business was thriving and Ryan was enjoying life once again.

They say five years is the amount of time, that if you make it, you will be clear of cancer. However, that was not to be the case for Ryan. I guess he was the exception to the rule. Almost five years later I got another phone call from Ryan to tell me that the cancer had in fact returned to his tongue. Once again, you could have scraped me off the sidewalk. This time the hurt in my chest felt more than I could bear. Ryan was facing surgery again. This was followed by both chemo and radiation this time. Ryan endured a significant amount of pain and discomfort from these processes. This time it did not heal as well as the first time and he required further surgery, this time to his neck. It was evident that the cancer was spreading. This also did not heal very well and it was further evident that the cancer was ravaging Ryan's body. Soon an open sore at the sight of the recent surgery was visual evidence the cancer was winning. It was difficult to be hopeful and optimistic at this point but we did our best. His chemo doctor was trying different treatments and different doses of chemo in order to control the cancer; he even used a drug trial. The choice was always Ryan's as to whether he wanted further treatment.

Nearly eight years after the initial diagnosis and while in hospital yet again, Ryan was told to get his affairs in order. It was heartbreaking to hear the words. Ryan was a trooper. He followed these orders. He made out his will and wrote down his last wishes. Despite this, he remained hopeful and he never complained. On one occasion I said to him that that I wished it was I that had cancer instead of him for I have had a longer time to enjoy life than he and his response was, "no, Mom."

Ryan knew that he was losing the battle of his life and he did not want to stay in the hospital. He asked his Dad if he could go to his house. It was quickly arranged and Ryan seemed much happier to be there. From then on that is where I visited him. He was also visited daily by a palliative care doctor and nurses assisting the doctor. That was where Ryan spent his final days. He had his family by his side when he finally lost the battle. It was a relief to all of us that he was no longer in such extreme pain. I was holding his hand and rubbing the new hair on his head when he drew his final breaths. I watched as his fingernails turned blue from the lack of oxygen. His heart continued to beat even after his last breath. The nurse said his youthful heart was very strong. She said to Ryan, "it's okay to let go now, Ryan."

He was thirty one years, ten months and twenty-one days old when he died. What a shame! What a loss! For someone to suffer so long and hard and die at such a young age with such a brilliant mind was a monumental catastrophe to his family and friends!

Three Years Later

This was a wonderful day for Lyndsey and Jon. It felt good to celebrate a happy occasion once again with both of our families.

This should have been one of the happiest days of my life. Our youngest son, Jon, got married to Lyndsey and it was a magnificent and very special occasion. But in our hearts we were all missing Ryan. He should have been there. Jon had a lapel pin designed with Ryan's initials on it so he, his brother and their Dad could wear it at the wedding showing that Ryan was with them in spirit. Derek was also wearing one of Ryan's t-shirts under his white shirt and tie. The t-shirt had a logo on it that said, "Is there any way we can speed this up?" Ryan was well known for his t-shirts with such saying on them. Other shirt sayings were: I read your e-mail, My computer goes down on me, Make 7 (on front) Up yours (on back), WTF, Strangers (with benefits), and We hate your hate. Ryan had a unique sense of humour.

This is Ryan's older brother, Derek, with Ryan's younger brother, Jon at the wedding.

This pin was designed by Jon and worn by Jon, Derek and their Father as a sign that Ryan was with us on that very special day. The second picture shows a close-up of the pin. People choose to remember in different ways.

I chose to wear a black onyx necklace and earring set with dragonflies, of course, as accessories to the wedding to show my remembrance of Ryan and that he was sadly missed.

I was the Mother of the groom and I wore a black onyx dragonfly necklace with matching earrings. That was my way of honouring Ryan and to show that I knew he would be with us in spirit. At the dinner in Derek's speech he made reference to Ryan by including him in his comments as follows: "I know Ryan would echo me in saying that I feel very lucky to have you as a brother, Jon. I am very proud of the person you have become and I am happy you have found Lyndsey. Lyndsey, although it seems like you have been a member of the family for a long time, it is great to officially have you as a sister-in-law. Congratulations you two!"

Also at the wedding, one of my great nieces, Jessica, gave me an aventurine gemstone with a gold dragonfly etched on it. She worked at a New Age store the day of the wedding and while helping a customer, she spied it and knew she had to buy it and bring it to the wedding reception to give to me. What did it mean to me? Ryan made Jessica notice the stone; she gave it to me so that I would know that Ryan **was** at the wedding. This is an example of synchronicity and not a coincidence. For one thing I have learned through all my reading is that there are no coincidences. There will be more about that later. You need to be open to the **signs** from your loved one in order to receive these messages. Your **intuition** will tell you if you are correct. Before Ryan became so sick he talked about getting married and having a family someday. But that was not to be.

Through one of my psychic encounters, Ryan told me that although he did not have that opportunity, that he would get married and raise a family vicariously through Jon. Therefore, Jon should know that Ryan will be watching over him closely as he raises his family. Ryan will be there.

Who Was Ryan?

First of all, he was my son. He had two brothers; Derek was his older brother and Jon was his younger brother. He also had two step-sisters Vicki and Charlene and one step brother, Rob. Ryan was the fifth in order of age from oldest to youngest of the group of six in our family. Ryan lived in a blended family for most of his time at home and they got along amazingly well.

He was always a well behaved, lovable and curious child and an excellent student. He was offered the opportunity to attend a special school for gifted students but he declined because he did not want to leave his friends. He received many awards at his grade eight graduation. He was the kind of student who always had his assignments completed ahead of time and he was often seeking enrichment material to answer his curiosity particularly in the computer field. I remember in high school his computer teacher suggested to me that I buy him an advanced program which was another computer language and study it on his own as an extracurricular activity to satisfy his hunger for new information. He was also selected to be in a board wide band for York Region (north of Toronto) when he was in high school.

At times, it frustrated him that his younger brother, Jon, was a natural when it came to sports and it was a struggle for him to have to learn the various sports. But he was willing to participate. He found more satisfaction in skiing, golfing and in-line skating.

Ryan attended high school in Renfrew with his brother Jon. His older brother Derek was eight and a half years older, so he was on to university followed by a career in chemical engineering at this time. Ryan continued his education at Ottawa University in Ottawa where he studied computers, first the hardware and then specializing in software. What could I say when he phoned to say he was changing his major? I always told the boys if they chose a field in their career that they loved, it would not seem like work when they went to work each day.

When Ryan created his own company, the last big thing he was working on was "ruby-on rails" which was a new custom software program at the time. He was busy teaching it to friends and acquaintances in Ottawa. He was hired by SAP one of the largest software companies in the world to speak to their people at a conference in Las Vegas. They found him through his blog. It gave Ryan great satisfaction to be a player in this development in the bigger picture.

I googled Ryan recently and found many computer technology information pages that I could not begin to understand. See "non-Fattening Syntactic Sugar" page 4 to see how smart he really was. Just for fun, he has some sites that are rather humorous, ie) coffee vs. coke. I just found a site called, "Four Kinds of People." It is a four line entry as follows:

Those who make things happen
Those to whom thing happen
Those who watch things happen
Those who don't even know things are happening.

It is a blog and people add their comments. I am gaining insight into a side of Ryan that I was never privy to know until now. As one blogger added, "we are always those four people simultaneously," but for the most part, I know that Ryan was one who made things happen in the computer software world in Ottawa, Ontario.

Reflections From
His Older Brother

I still remember when I was eight years old and Dad came to me to tell me that he and Mom had something to tell me. For some reason, I asked, "Is Mom pregnant?" From that day on I knew that a little brother or sister was on the way. I was so excited! I had been an only child all my life, so I was really looking forward to a sibling to play with. From the day that they brought Ryan home, I wanted to hold him and play with him as much as I could.

I think the age difference brought me closer to Ryan (and our younger brother, Jon, afterwards) than I would have been, since I learned to change his diapers, feed him and otherwise take care of him. I got to earn a bit of money but we always had lots of fun playing Nerf hockey in the hallway, watching all the kids' TV shows for which they knew all the theme songs and all the commercials by heart and just generally hanging out. I didn't realize until years later that I was as much a young parent to them as I was an older brother. That was until they got older and realized that I had gone through all the things they were going through with girls, school, and life, in general, and that I could offer them 'older brother advice'.

Ryan was a self-described 'weird dude' but he was one of the most talented computer developers that I have ever worked with. He tried the nine-to-five work thing and decided it wasn't for him. He decided instead to be a consultant and only work on projects that he wanted to work on and only work enough to pay his bills.

I only found out after his death from his friends and colleagues just how selfless he was with his time. He was always willing to help a friend or new acquaintance that had a (usually technical) question or problem.

There was no shortage of stories about Ryan helping people and the effect that he had on his friends was made even more clear than I read all of the postings on his Facebook memorial page on his 34th birthday, even three years after his death.

I miss Ryan every day. And I am still angry that he was taken away from us so early but also glad to have the time with him that I did. I have some of my favourite pictures of him up on my walls and I still wear some of his well-known t-shirts sometimes; I feel closer to him as well as being in my thoughts. When I get together with family, we often reminisce about 'what Ryan would do or say' or things that he had done. I have many fond memories of Ryan and some of them are in my speech at his funeral.

Derek's Speech

While Ryan and I had spent every day together when he was young, due to our age difference we had not spent as much time together since I went away to university when he was ten. There were, however, sometimes we did spend together that I would like to share with you. Ryan, Jon and I had the opportunity to spend a week in Barbados to celebrate their respective graduations from university. Ryan was in great physical shape then, as well as confident and carefree. That week was one of the highlights of my life, with all three brothers being able to spend quality time together as adults. Although some of our actions may have led people to question that status. That is how I will remember Ryan.

When Ryan graduated from Engineering, I had the privilege of presenting Ryan with his Iron Ring. At the ceremony, he said the oath, I put the ring on his finger, he gave me a hug and the moment was quickly over. I knew he appreciated it and it was a special moment for both of us. Ryan then shook my hand and before he went back to his seat, he said, "We are almost done, so we can go and get a beer soon. Until then, don't bother any of the women in the gallery", deflecting from the brief seriousness of the moment. That is how I will remember Ryan.

While I knew that Ryan was really good at what he did for a living, developing websites, I hadn't seen much of it for myself as many of his projects were very secretive. In the last couple of years we had the opportunity to partner on a project. Once we decided what we wanted the site to do, it wasn't long before he made that happen and more. Another example was a few years ago, SAP, one of the largest software companies in the world, found Ryan through his blogs and paid him to go to Las Vegas to speak to their people about Ruby on Rails, a relatively new computer language at the time. It was at this point that I started to understand the level of Ryan's ability. That is how I remember Ryan.

All along, Ryan has handled his situation with dignity and without ever complaining. When Jon and I visited him at his apartment with Dad, he seemed more concerned about us than he did with himself. Despite the fact that he was not eating much at the time and he was clearly uncomfortable, he wanted to make sure that he gave Jon advice on getting internet service set up at his new house so he didn't pay too much or get subpar service.

Also, out of the blue, Ryan said to us, "I am about 130 pounds right now, I have you both beat." We all had running weight jokes over the years with each of us always trying to lose or gain weight. So, we knew Ryan had not lost his sense of humour. When I sensed that Ryan was getting a bit tired, I said, "Well, we should go. I am getting a bit hungry and I promised Jon some supper". Ryan's response was "and here I am eating a Jello right in front of you." It was one of the few things he managed to eat that day. Even in his current situation, he found time for humour. That is how I will remember Ryan.

One night more recently at Dad's in Ryan's final days, as I was holding a cool cloth to his head, he opened his eyes suddenly. Sometimes that was just a reflex so we weren't sure if he was actually awake. When this happened I always said, "Hi Ryan".

This time he said "hey" back. I told him it was me and asked him if it was okay if I sat with him. He said, "ya".

I said "I love you Ryan" and he said "I love you too".

That was the last conversation that I had with Ryan. My most recent time with Ryan has shown me a lot about the person he had become, as has seeing and speaking with many of you. It has made me even more proud to have had him as a brother. I love you Ryan. We all love you. Derek

This photo was the last one to be taken of the three brothers. They were attending a cousin's wedding. They are from left to right: Jon, Ryan and Derek.

Reflections from his
Younger Brother

Ryan's presence in my life was never really fully realized until after he was gone. He was always just 'there'. That sounds worse than it actually is, so I'll try to explain. I've got literally thousands of memories involving him; none of which I can say are bad. I don't think I could come up with one scenario where I was wronged by my brother; he was just that kind of guy. He was a blend-into-the background, go-with-the-flow type of person. He didn't make waves, he didn't crave attention, and if the girls didn't think he was so damn good looking, he wouldn't have stood out at all. From a very early age I always looked to Ryan for intelligent advice. He was always smarter than me, always a lot more cautious and usually much more reserved. If I was about to do something stupid, he would tell me. He wouldn't stop me but he would tell me. Consider it more an opportunity to tell me "I told you so" when something went wrong, or to tell Mom "I told him not to do it", when we got in trouble.

Ryan and I were the closest in age and also the youngest two in a large blended family of six children. We spent a lot of time in our younger days making up our own games and acting out our own little adventures. Actually, I didn't do much making up, I pretty much let him tell me what we were doing and I went along with it. Thinking back now, I can remember building snow forts in Pakenham, building cities with Meccano and Construx in Newmarket, riding our bikes, swimming and skiing together and skiing at about every ski hill around where we lived. Neither one of us turned out to be very good skiers though. We played road hockey, hide and seek, kick the can, baseball and all sorts of other games with the rest of the kids in the neighbourhood, especially the Mattingleys.

We grew up in a very kid-friendly, well-populated community. I think I spent most of my days outside from the time I was in grade two until about grade eight, but not Ryan. From the very first time Mom brought that first 286 computer home, Ryan was glued to it. I had to beg him to come outside and play and eventually I just stopped asking. I remember the kids in the court would actually get excited when he would come outside because he was a lot of fun. The problem was that it didn't happen that often. I actually think Mom had to force him to go outside some days. The computer was his passion and that continued right up until the day he died. He was never more than an arm's length from a computer and eventually an internet connection.

When we moved to Renfrew and to a new high school, I remember being worried about him because although we both started a new school, he started in grade ten. By grade ten friendship circles were already established. People around Renfrew knew everybody. It seemed like they were all related to each other one way or another. Ryan's cure for this was that he just picked a table that he thought the "cool" kids were at in the cafeteria and he sat down. Literally he just sat down and ate his lunch; it still blows my mind. He continued to do this day after day and eventually earned himself the nickname 'New Guy'. They eventually just got used to him being around. I can't imagine the courage it would have taken to pull a stunt like that and I never asked him about it. When I first learned how he met his Renfrew friends, I often wondered what his grade nine experiences must have been like in Newmarket. He was a thin, blonde-haired geek with a mushroom cut that was WAAAAY into computers, science and band. He must have been terrorized. He never talked about grade nine, and again I didn't ask. When we moved to Renfrew he dropped a lot of his nerdiness but he kept his love for computers. He certainly didn't join the band.

As an adult, I can clearly say that all of my time spent with my brother was time well spent. We had an interesting and not-so conventional relationship to say the least. When we were in university I did not get to see him very much but he always called, e-mailed or ICQed me to make sure I was doing okay. He gave me advice on how and what to study for exams and he was my go-to person for computer issues. He wasn't much help though because he preferred walk-throughs instead of quick fixes. I learned a lot through that method which I am sure was his plan all along. The more he taught me the less I would call him with problems that needed his expertise. This reflects the whole 'give a man a pole' or 'teach a man to fish' analogy. I'm sure you know them.

I spent a lot of time with Ryan as a young adult. He actually lived with me for a year or so. We went to hockey games, concerts, parties, bars or anything at all. They were usually always his picking and his friends. He liked my friends, don't get me wrong, but I can count on one hand the number of times that he came out with us somewhere. Ryan had an interesting way of organizing his friends into little groups (I believe my stepmom called them "buckets'). For certain events he hung out with certain people and most of these people were unaware the other groups existed. The best example I can give you is the surprised look on their faces when the good-looking girl in the red dress spoke at his funeral. People were thinking "Who is that?" There was one constant in Ryan's groups of friends though. Every single person that ever became part of his inner circle was a dear friend and one he kept forever. He might not call, write or see them very often but when he did call them they were always there for him and vice-versa. This fact was made much clearer for me when I finally had to go against his direction and tell his friends that he was dying. Most of them didn't even know he was sick in the first place let alone sick with terminal cancer. It was tough for everyone and I knew he didn't want me to say anything but they needed to know and I am sure he was glad they did know when they showed up at the door to visit in his final days. The number of people that showed up to support our family at the wakes and funeral was staggering . . . absolutely mind blowing. I think that seeing all those people that cared for him helped my parents cope quite a bit as well.

I've been avoiding talking about his illness much, so I guess I will address the obvious issue. I was devastated when he first told me about his cancer; I was absolutely crushed. My first thought was, "Oh no, you are going to die." He assured me that that wasn't the case at all and that it was no big deal. There would be treatments and things would get better. It never did. Until he died though, he handled his whole situation with dignity, grace and in a way 99% of the world would (and could) not. He certainly did not embrace death but he understood his situation. He knew his illness, he researched his treatments and he knew that when he left the hospital for the last time against his doctor's advice, he wouldn't be back. I never heard him complain once. I never thought in a million years that the cancer would beat him. I remember the day he told me he wasn't going to beat it. I remember crying in the hospital and telling him that I did not want to live without my brother. He told me that he did not want to live without me either. He told me to be strong, that things would be okay, and that I had a great woman that would be with me forever. He told me that he loved me, that he was proud of me and proud of the life that I had made for myself.

When he died, we were all there: Mom, Dad, Derek, Bob, Maria and Lyndsey. The family that been broken apart years before was momentarily back together. If you have never seen someone you love die, it is very surreal. I certainly don't recommend it. In that moment, as uncomfortable as it was, I wouldn't want to be anywhere else. There he was just a skeleton of his former self. He was once a fit, muscular young body. Now there was nothing more than skin holding in whatever parts of his body that were still working, albeit poorly. I still remember how much NOT like Ryan he looked. If you looked long enough you could convince yourself that it wasn't him, but it was. When he took his final breath, I thought,' I'm glad, so glad that's over". I don't know if that is normal behavior or not. The relief I felt was unlike anything I've experienced before. He didn't deserve to suffer, or to be in pain, or to live like that. I was totally relieved when he passed away. The brother that I loved wouldn't suffer anymore.

In the days and weeks that passed (and in the days leading up to his death), I watched my family struggle with a lot of things. For most of his life, Ryan kept himself purposefully at a distance from just about everyone, except me it seems. I was a little luckier than most, I guess. Maybe because I was his only younger brother or maybe because I was his best friend, I'm not sure. He always did his best to make sure I was involved in everything he was doing and he always kept in close contact with me. I was privy to all areas and aspects of his life. He kept nothing from me. That closeness allowed me to have absolutely no regrets when Ryan passed away. I had spent as much time as I could or that he would allow with him. I had met everyone he wanted me to meet. I had done everything he had asked me to do. I didn't have trouble coping with his death because I was okay with it. I had talked to him about it beforehand. He had given me the older brotherly advice that I needed to move forward with my own life. He told me to lean on Lyndsey Frances Cameron and I did. She was there for me every step of the way. I'm not sure how I would have coped without her, but I don't need to wonder, she was there. Ryan had always made her feel like part of his family too, so we mourn for him in our own little way.

Nowadays, I keep myself going by thinking of all the ridiculous stuff we used to get into. His pictures hang on the wall in our living room. My memories are nothing but positive. His Facebook page, along with his memorial page, gets updated every now and then by thoughts his friends share and stories they tell about things they did with him. Seeing all that love and experiencing what other people thought of him helps a lot. I jump on when I can, usually around his birthday or the anniversary of the day he died and throw my own memories into the mix. I try to come up with things that he and I shared that other people wouldn't necessarily know. I think it helps us all.

Was he taken from us too soon? Yes. Did he deserve to die? No, he didn't. Do I miss him? More than I could ever explain in words. Am I okay with how my life with him before and after his passing has gone? Yes, I am. I can say with 100% certainty, that wherever he is, and whatever he is doing, he's proud of me. He always was. And that helps.

How Do You Survive?

How does one go on after the loss of your son, daughter or loved one? I can only say how I survived that first year. I think the word "numb" pretty well sums it up. Or perhaps, I would consider I was in automatic pilot. The only thing I can think of is that I had a spouse and two other sons to live for and three step children as well as four siblings of my own who would miss me if I were not to survive. So I got up each day, put one foot in front of the other trying to be as normal as I could possibly be. Some days I was only pretending and always seemingly wearing a mask in order to pull that off.

Shortly after Ryan's passing, we went to Florida. A couple of days after arriving, a neighbor, Janet, came over to express her sympathy and handed me a book by John Edwards, a psychic medium who also hosts a TV show called Crossing Over. Janet invited me to watch it with her. He talked to deceased relatives and the people were totally amazed at the accuracy of the personal information he relayed to them. It captivated me. A week later, I picked up a number of books at a local bookstore, this time the author was Sylvia Browne. Her first book that I read was "Blessings from the Other Side". It was an easy read and really made me start to think. These two books were the start of my thirst for more information about dying, death and the afterlife. One of the things I learned is that we should try to get a sign from our loved one before he or she dies so that when we see that sign we think of them and know that they are thinking of us in return in spirit. I was sad that I did not know this before Ryan's passing, so how was I going to have a sign for him? I was deeply saddened that I did not have a sign from him. In the last months he did not want to talk about dying.

Try to get a sign from your loved one to remind you of him/her.

A few days later, when I turned on my computer, I realized that he HAD left me a sign. On the sign in page both of our names appeared with a logo. My sign was a gingerbread man (I'll never know why he chose that for me) and his sign was a dragonfly. You see, I bought a Laptop computer and allowed Ryan to use it when he was no longer able to sit up at his desk to use his computer for any length of time. He could use the laptop while lying on the couch. He set it up and used it for a while to make sure it was working alright, he said. It was just a little thing; but each time I saw a dragonfly after that, whether it was on my computer, someone's jewelry or on a garden ornament, it warmed my heart a little and made me smile. I know I thought of Ryan each time and I believed that he was responsible for me noticing the dragonfly in whatever form. I started recording my sightings and in the first year I quickly recorded over two hundred different dragonflies in novel and surprising places. I did not count the ones that I expected to find, only the ones that took me by surprise. Let me share a few with you.

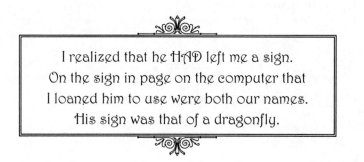

I realized that he HAD left me a sign.
On the sign in page on the computer that
I loaned him to use were both our names.
His sign was that of a dragonfly.

I went to a white elephant sale in the park where we live and a lady had a tattoo of a dragonfly on her ankle. I told her I liked her tattoo and she said, "Then you are going to like my t-shirt too." It had about twenty other dragonflies on it in many beautiful colours.

I went to a store called "Ross Dress For Less" and I was trying on shoes and noticed that the lining in a pair that I was trying on had dragonflies on them. Go figure!

While at a garden center looking for flowers to plant, I spied a huge metal dragonfly about three feet wide. I bought it of course and it graces the gable of out two car garage back in Renfrew, Ontario.

One that really caught us by surprise was when we went on a cruise and stopped at San Juan. As we got off the ship the sight-seeing tour guides were waiting for passengers. On the uniform of the very first guide was a dragonfly as the logo for the company, 'Dragonfly Tours'. We decided that Ryan came along on the cruise with us. We continued to do a walking tour of the downtown and Bob stopped me and said to get my camera ready. I asked him what for and soon realized that it was to take the picture of a very large restaurant sign with a dragonfly on it. It served Latinasian food and it was a suishi bar. After those two sightings we decided Ryan was definitely on the trip with us! Please remember that you must be open to the **signs** from spirit. They are always trying to get your attention and make you think of them.

The uniform of the first guide had a dragonfly on it for the logo of the tour company, Dragonfly Tours.

A very large sign for a restaurant had a huge dragonfly on it.

The next summer we went on a short trip to Newfoundland. We went into a museum and gift shop and of course I checked out a beautiful display of homemade quilts. Since I am a quilter, I checked out the workmanship and the backing of each quilt. You guessed it. One of them had dragonflies over the entire backing.

On a short shopping trip to Balderson, my friend Joanne and I spent a few hours checking out the clothes, the crafts and gifts in the shops and discovered many dragonflies as we expected. But we came across an entire set of pottery dishes hand made by a crafter and of course the dragonfly was on every piece. What a delightful find!

Friends began to know what a dragonfly sighting meant for me and they soon started showing me dragonflies that they owned. My sister-in-law, Cheryl, showed me a beautiful brooch that her son had given her for Christmas. It was a Swarovski crystal pin.

My Good friend, Ilse, showed me a stained glass dragonfly that she had placed at the base of a potted tree in her screened in porch in Florida. She has had it there for a couple of years, but has just recently noticed it again.

Bob B. told me about a solar set of garden lights and one of them was a dragonfly. Shortly after, one appeared in my garden from guess who?

Bob's daughter, Vicki, (my step daughter) came for a visit in Florida and before going home presented us with a set of crystal wine glasses with dragonfly etchings on them. What a beautiful gift. It meant a lot that she understood that this gift was helping me to heal.

Vicki presented us with a lovely pair of crystal wine glasses with dragonflies etched on them. Thank you, Vicki.

My son, Jon, does not really "get" what seeing a dragonfly does for me, but Lyndsey (his wife) says, "Whatever works". They have given me a purple wind catcher hanging and a garden ornament. I appreciate that they are going along with me on this dragonfly phase.

I have seen a number of dragonfly sightings on TV too. While watching the news, the anchor lady was wearing the most beautiful necklace with a large dragonfly as the center stone. You couldn't miss it. Sometimes the sightings are at the right time to perk up my spirits.

I watched a movie called "Fly Me to the Moon" in which the opening scene was a swamp and a dragonfly the size of the entire screen flew across. I didn't know if it was part of the movie or whether Ryan was playing tricks on me. Apparently spirits can manipulate anything electronic to suit their desires.

Another movie was called "Dragonfly" in which Kevin Kostner was trying to communicate with his dead wife through the drawings of a dragonfly of one of her patients. She was pregnant before going on a trip to work as a doctor and she led him to the location of their child after much searching.

Bob and I were in the habit of watching "Two and a Half Men" before we went to bed. We used to like to watch a comedy because it made us laugh. It helps to heal to laugh. Charlie's Mother was always dressed in a suit and one night she wore a large sparkly dragonfly brooch. I was beginning to think that Ryan was planting these sightings because he knew we always watch this show.

On Grey's Anatomy, a doctor show, two doctors were standing in the hall discussing a case and guess what the picture was in the background. I almost phoned someone to see if they saw the dragonfly picture too in the background or was Ryan still playing his games. Either way, I was both surprised and delighted to notice it.

Enough already; I think you get the picture by now.

I have to tell you that not only did I have sightings of dragonflies, but friends and relatives started giving me gifts with dragonflies on them because they knew how much they meant to me. The giving continues even after three years since he passed away.

What I want you to get from all this is that it helped me in the beginning to have that sign. If you want a sign from your loved one then you will have to have a conversation while they are still with you and ask them for one. If this is not likely to happen, then I suggest that you can pick a sign that reminds you of him or her and that person (in spirit) will know that you chose it for them. After all, they are spirits and they know these things. They like to be remembered and they like you to think of them often. Personally, it eased the suffering a little because I believe that Ryan is still with me.

Over the first three years after Ryan's passing, I have immersed myself in reading and researching such topics as dying, death, Reiki, the afterlife, spirits, angels, reincarnation and past lives. Sometimes, I went on little tangents because the topic seemed related and interesting at the time. Some of these topics were hypnosis, astrology, numerology and yoga to name a few. It helped me to really get to know and internalize some this amazing information.

Mysterious Happenings

A loved one who has passed will often let you know that they are alright or tell you something else in your dreams. Shortly after Ryan passed, I had a dream where Ryan said to me, "I will help you through this." He looked the picture of health in my dream which is what I have read in a number of the books that I have read. This statement was followed by a wonderful long hug and when he moved away, he turned into my youngest son, Jon. I took this to mean that I should look after Jon to help him through this loss as well.

On another morning about 5:30 a.m. I dreamt that someone was massaging my neck and shoulders. No one was around at the time. I am convinced it was Ryan. One book said that spirits can reach out to you in the physical realm. It is hard work for them but if you are in a relaxed state such as early morning sleep, they can meet you half way.

One evening I went to bed before Bob. He was in the bathroom brushing his teeth and I felt someone gently touch my left hip. I looked around and there was no one there. I asked Bob if he touched me. His response was negative. I KNOW that it was Ryan that touched me. I don't know how I know, I just know. This concurs with my reading as well.

On another evening Bob fell asleep almost immediately as usual; I felt someone softly touch my forehead like a kiss. I believe that that, too, was Ryan giving me kiss.

I am not the only one who is pretty sure that Ryan was with her. Ryan's step-sister Vicki, who works for CTV, went to a concert because it was two of Ryan's favorite bands. She went alone but during the concert someone touched her shoulder. She looked around but nobody she knew was near her. She was convinced that Ryan touched her and watched the concert with her.

When Ryan was very sick in the hospital and before I went to visit him, I always played a particular hymn every day before I travelled down to Ottawa to see him. It was called, "Fly like a Bird". Once I got to Florida I went too many days without a sign that Ryan was around. Before I went to sleep that evening I asked Ryan to give me a sign the next day that he was still with me. The next morning we went to Church and during communion the choir sang that hymn. I am sure the people around me were wondering why I was crying. Bob put his arm around me; he knew what I was thinking. What a strong sign. Spirits are able to make some amazing things happen. I certainly got my sign that day!

Another unbelievable story involves my good friend Betty, also now deceased. She phoned me one day and said I had to go to her house so she could tell me something. I asked her to tell me on the phone but she was insistent that

I should go to her house to talk to her. When I arrived she seemed extremely agitated. She began her story saying that she could not sleep well that night and she kept hearing a voice saying, "Go to Cobden". That is a small town about twenty minutes from her home. After hearing this multiple times, she went to the bathroom to wash her face with cold water. She went back to bed and continued to hear the voice say the same thing, "Go to Cobden." At seven o'clock in the morning she called another friend and asked her what to do. Her friend said to go to Cobden. So Betty hopped in her car and headed for Cobden. While on her way she once more heard, "Go to Cobden". This time she had a response for the voice. She said aloud, "I AM going to Cobden". She said by now she just knew it was Ryan's voice even thought she had never even met him nor heard his voice. When she entered the town of Cobden, she stopped the car at the side of the road and said aloud, "what now?" She looked around and decided she should go to the Celtic Gift Shop, still wondering why. She perused the store and eventually came to the jewelry display. While looking at the display she gasped. The saleslady asked her if anything was wrong and Betty answered that something was very right. Before her eyes was a brooch with two dragonflies on it. It was adorned with pink stones. One dragonfly was larger than the other. The saleslady said, "Oh, that is the Mother and Son pin" and Betty knew immediately why she was sent to Cobden. As soon as she returned home, she phoned me to come and visit her. Ryan had reached out to my very good friend who also believes in angels and spirits to send me yet another very special message. Once Betty handed me the pin, she calmed right down having completed her mission. What an amazing story! Remember there are no coincidences and you must be open to receive these messages.

The pin with the two dragonflies is the one that Betty gave to me. The clerk called it the Mother and son pin.

One more thing that many people would find very strange is that since Ryan passed, I have been able to smell a scent that reminds me of him. When he was sick, there was a distinct smell around when you walked into his room. That is the same smell that I would get initially about two dozen times a day after he passed. The frequency waned after many months to now where I only get the smell occasionally. Perhaps that is because I now believe he is with me all the time. He knows how often I think of him or am reminded of him by so many triggers. Apparently spirits like to be thought of frequently. So Ryan must be very pleased with me.

Eventually, other smells permeated the room from time to time. I began to believe other spirits were paying me a visit because they knew I was open to the spirit world. I smelled Ryan's smell frequently for a whole year so it was very easy to discriminate his from any other that may visit. I was wondering if it might be my Mom or Dad, either of my grandparents or friends who have crossed over. I still haven't figured that out yet. But one evening when I was receiving quite a distinctive smell I said out loud, "who is visiting me?" I was watching a western on television and there was a saloon and it was called "Hanks". Usually a saloon is called the Silver Dollar Saloon, Lucky Lady or the name of the town's saloon. What was unusual about the name is that one of my psychics had told me that I had a spirit guide called Hank. So I guess I now know his smell too. Apparently I am the only one who smells these smells because I have asked Bob if he ever did and his answer was always no.

Remember to **be open** to ANYTHING!

"WHEN YOU CHANGE THE WAY YOU LOOK AT THINGS, THE THINGS YOU LOOK AT CHANGE."

Books Helped

Only weeks after Ryan died, I started my quest for information on dying and the afterlife. I literally buried myself in books soaking up all the information that rang true to my beliefs and understanding. I have read over one hundred and twenty books and some of them twice because they were so interesting and I wanted to make sure I digested the material. It was very interesting how some books would just stood out and caught my attention one after another to help me on my journey of understanding and hopefully help me heal along the path. This is called synchronicity. It didn't seem to matter whether I was in a used book store or a book store that only sold new ones; I always found some that interested me at the time. Reading became my new and exclusive hobby that opened the door to an understanding of my situation and led me to activities that I could take part in to heal myself and perhaps help others. I am specifically referring to **Reiki** (a form of hands on healing) and the use of angel cards. I started receiving Reiki treatments from Heather because I read that it would be an effective way to heal myself by getting a treatment from a qualified person and eventually giving myself a treatment.

Reiki is a safe and gentle hands-on healing procedure for you or to administer to others. It uses spiritual energy to treat physical maladies as well as spiritual and emotional. It is also a holistic method to balance, heal and harmonize your body, mind and spirit. It is believed that if the energy centers of the body are blocked then you will develop a disease. Every negative thought or word can affect the energy centers of your body. In converse, every positive thought, word or sighting will raise your vibration and help you in being healthy and well. When experiencing a Reiki treatment the high frequency healing energy will accelerate the body's own natural healing ability. It is guided by a higher wisdom and always works for the highest good of the person receiving it; it cannot be harmful in any way. So it is a win-win technique.

While there, Heather always had me choose an angel card. It was always relevant to my needs at that particular time and heightened my interest. I found a number of card decks at the local New Age store called "Soul Scents" in Almonte and started to do my own **angel cards** on a daily basis. I now own four decks of cards and continue to do them daily and on occasion I will do them for someone else if they are interested.

It was intriguing how one book often lead to another and sometimes interested me in other related topics like hypnosis, gemstone and crystal therapy, feng shei, yoga and aromatherapy. But to date the two areas that interest me the most are Reiki and Angel cards. I have subsequently taken training from Heather and I am a Master Reiki Practitioner/ Teacher. Both make me feel much better.

I have learned a great deal through my reading and I have internalized a lot of information that rang true for me. You should do the same. Some things you will believe or want to believe and that is what you should take from it. Your own **intuition** or "gut feeling" will tell you what rings true for you. Some of my favorite authors are: Sylvia Browne, John Edwards, James Van Praagh, Doreen Virtue, Sonia Choquette, Brian Weiss and Ruth Montgomery.

Everyone Is Different

People are going to grieve differently. What worked for me may not work for you all the time. What works for you today may not work for you tomorrow. Only you will know what will work for you. Emotions run rampant and you will feel like you are on an emotional roller coaster. The triggers are everywhere in your day to day living. For example, a picture of tulips is a really strong trigger for me because when Ryan was quite sick and he still lived in his apartment, we went for a stroll through the gardens of the Ottawa Tulip Festival. He only lived a couple of blocks from the gardens. When I see tulips or pictures of them, I think of Ryan and I am reminded of the constant pain in my heart and at the same time I have a happy memory of him and the two of us sharing a very special time together. When I drive past the local high school I think of both Jon and Ryan. I think of the fact that Ryan is no longer with us. My old 2000 Grand Prix is a trigger. Jon has it now but I loaned it to Ryan to go to get groceries, go to yoga, massage therapy or doctors' appointments before he was very sick. Sometimes I drive it and think of Ryan sitting in the very same seat. Of course Ryan comes to mind every time I see a similar car while I am out driving. I am constantly reminded of him while watching TV. When I see an Apple commercial or computers, Iphones or when I see cop shows when they use computers to solve crimes I think of Ryan. I am here to tell you that Ryan is constantly on my mind and your loved one will be on your mind all the time too. I don't find it upsetting; I would rather see it as a gift that helps me to remember him. I was grateful that he was in my life even if the time together was too short.

There are hundreds of triggers for me daily and there will be for you too. It is how you handle them that dictate how you will survive the various situations. There will be times when there is a trigger for you but not the other person and they will be oblivious to the fact that you are having a mini meltdown. There will be times when the moment will be overwhelming and you will excuse yourself and find a quiet place to recover or choose to go home. At times the tears are right there waiting to fall. That's when a friend or family member takes the cues from the grieving person and follows their lead. If the person wants to cry, let them. If the person wants to talk, let them. Their job is to just be there and listen. If the person wants to be strong and be in control of the situation follow their lead and gently change the subject when you feel it is a good time to interject with a new topic.

Their job is to just be there and listen.

I found out I was in different emotional levels each day especially soon after Ryan passed. Some days I just wanted to stay in my pyjamas for the day and watch movies or go from one activity to another holed up in my home. I knew this was not the best strategy but I found that if I did this when I needed to I had the strength to get up the next day, get dressed and do something a little more productive or social. But I have to tell you that when I went out it was like putting on a mask and pretending that I was fine. At least it was in the right direction to get on with life even if it was only a baby step. There was a lot of role playing in the early days. There were many days when I had to go to town for some groceries and I hoped that I would not run in to anyone I knew because I did not want to talk to anyone. The same was true when we went to Church. This is where I am reminded how thankful I was for having a very supportive husband for the worst days of my life. He would listen to me when I did want to talk about Ryan. He would allow me to jabber on about happy memories of Ryan. He would suggest activities that we could do together to get my mind off Ryan and distract me with such activities as boating, a drive or a movie. He would take most phone calls so I would not have to talk to anyone unless I wanted to. Members of my family were very good too although they may not know how much they really helped. I have three sisters and a brother and they all have significant others. I would often drive and hour each way to spend some time with them just to hang out together. I just needed to be with family, to be with people that love me. They are not as forward as I am about talking about dying and death. I would ramble on talking about Ryan and they would let me. I recognized the look in their eyes of the fear of not knowing what to say back but they didn't need to say anything. They just needed to LISTEN. I just continued to talk including Ryan in the conversation as if he were still alive and I believe they got used to me including him in our conversations. They probably did not know it at the time but they were helping me heal and get through this most difficult time together. Thank you to all of you. You know who you are.

My siblings. From left to right are Benita, Joe, Peggy, Mary and me at a family gathering.

Charlene is Ryan's stepsister and she chose to remember Ryan by designing and getting a tattoo of Ryan's name on her ankle.

Charlene chose to remember Ryan by tattooing his name on her ankle. What a great tribute to your brother, Char!

Jon has a collage of pictures of Ryan hanging in his living room.

Derek has a number of Ryan's t-shirts and wears them from time to time. He also has his glasses and case on display as well as photos on his wall.

Was God Responsible?

I'm sure everyone who has lost a loved one has asked why God would do this to them. I know I did. What did your loved one do to deserve this? What did I do to deserve this? Could I have done anything different? Of course I know I asked all of these questions and more. I prayed for the entire eight years that Ryan would beat his cancers. I seemed to be praying all the time. It didn't matter if I was driving in the car, doing housework or gardening; I was praying. But it did not work for Ryan. I just guess that Ryan and God had a different plan. We will never know why. That is, until we too go to the **Other Side**; then we will know once and for all. When Ryan did lose his battle I was definitely angry with God. How could he take Ryan at thirty-one years of age? Ryan was just beginning a very promising career. Because of my faith and after much thought, I decided I needed God more than ever to pull me out of this one. I continued going to Church and asked Him to help me heal and figure out how I can honour Ryan in some way. To this day, God is a very important part of my life as I continue to learn more about spirits, angels and the afterlife. It is both surprising and comforting to say that my new found knowledge does not contradict the teachings in my Church of choice (Catholic), as far as I can see, nor does it many other religions. As a matter of fact it clarifies a lot of the readings and Gospels that are part of the Mass.

I have not prayed so much in my life. At the initial diagnosis I prayed that the surgery would be successful and it was for five years. When the cancer came back and he had surgery again I prayed for the same outcome again. This time he had chemo and radiation so I was praying that they would be sufficient and that the toll would not be too difficult for Ryan. But then he had an open sore on his neck and surgery on his neck was in order, I was realizing that Ryan's cancer was definitely winning over his body and my prayers were definitely not working. So then I changed my prayers so that he would have a peaceful death and not a dramatic one because we knew that the tentacles of the cancer were wrapped around his carotid artery. At this point the prognosis was not optimistic. Ryan never knew that I was praying for anything but a cure.

The last two months of Ryan's battle I took a little vial of holy water with me when I visited him. Early in each visit I would make the sign of the cross on his forehead three times. On one occasion, I guess I did not do it fast enough because he asked me if I brought "the stuff" with me that day. I smiled and promptly performed my ritual on him. You should know that Ryan did not attend church as an adult. Near the end, Ryan did not want to see a priest or talk to any Chaplin at the hospital. At the very least I decided to re-baptize Ryan. I learned as a child that lay persons could baptize others in an emergency. I decided that baptism by his own Mother might ensure him entry into Heaven. You should realize I was rather desperate and would try anything. What harm would it do? It may have served some purpose because in Ryan's last will and testament he wrote that he wanted to be buried in a Catholic cemetery. I know he did that for me. I arranged that and was permitted to arrange the funeral service as well, also in the Catholic Church in Almonte, where he was born.

I still pray for Ryan as well as talk to him on a regular basis. I learned in studying catechism as a child that you should pray for people after they die. It is rather like a bank account of grace. It allows him to get close to God. Each morning and evening I say ten times the Lord's Prayer and often when I am driving the car. I say the Lord's Prayer because it is the greatest prayer that our Lord taught us Himself. When I go walking or biking it is another time to forward some more prayers. So if you have a loved one who has crossed over you should continue to pray for them too. They know we are praying for them and thinking of them.

I cannot talk about **prayer** without including readings from the **Bible**; for it is the greatest book of all time. You may gain some solace from becoming more familiar with the Bible. As a Catholic we did not study the Bible and memorize portions like some religions do. We became familiar with portions of it through the Readings and the Gospels that were a regular part of the Mass. Sometimes the priest would further explain the readings or the Gospel in his sermon. I have to say because of the extensive reading I have been doing those readings and Gospels are taking on clearer meanings. I find I am listening more intently to see if there is a particular message for me that day that I can apply to my daily life or as a message from Ryan or one of my other spirit guides. I think God is finally getting through to me on a deeper level.

I attended a Bible study group while in Florida. They happen to be studying Revelations. Since it is prophetic in nature I was curious to hear what Betty had to say about it.

You will gain comfort from a variety of sources and you have to decide what resonates for you. We are not all the same and we will gain different meanings from messages depending on our belief systems that we grew up with. The best way we can honour those that we have lost is to live our lives the best way we know how and live life to the fullest until it is our turn to join them in Heaven.

The best way to honour those that we have lost is to live our lives the best way we know how and live life to the fullest.

The following is a short poem read to us at a bible study meeting. It is meant to encourage us to live in the now, not the past or the future and that God is always with you.

MY NAME IS I AM

I was regretting the past and fearing the future.
Suddenly my Lord was speaking.
He paused. I waited. He continued:
"When you live in the past with its mistakes and regret, it is
hard.
I am not there. My name is not I WAS.
When you live in the future with its problems and fears, it
is hard.
I am not there. My name is not I WLL BE.
When you live in this moment, it is not hard. I am here. My
name is I AM."
He is always with you. You should talk to Him more often.
I do.

Alternative Healing

Ryan was the one who brought up the topic of alternative healing. He took yoga classes and went to massage therapy on a regular basis until it became too difficult for him to take part in these activities. He ate organic food as much as he could get his hands on. He mentioned to me one day that he wished he had had the opportunity to take part in alternative medicine but at that time I knew very little about it and I believe he realized it was too late for it to do any good for him. I thought perhaps this is one way **I** could honour Ryan and perhaps help someone else from my training. I decided to get trained in Reiki, a hands-on healing technique. Part 1 is so you can heal yourself and I certainly needed help in this department. I also offered sessions for friends or relatives back home in Canada if they were interested in trying it to see if they could benefit from it. There was a variety of responses from them. All participants said they felt heat from my hands. They all said they were much more relaxed after a session. Some said there was a part of their body that felt much better.

I truly believe that if you think it might help, it will. Some people believe in God or at least some kind of higher power. It is His power or power of the universe that channels through me to the client so they can heal themselves. I took Part 2 before I returned to Florida and found a few interested clients there during the winter. When I returned to Canada I took Part 3 and Masters. This was my goal before returning to Florida. I get something out of giving a treatment to someone. It is like the milk jug effect; there is always some milk left in the jug when you empty it. So, I get a residual effect of the Reiki for me. Also I am continuing to do Reiki on myself because even though it has been three years, I still need help to heal. I truly believe that life will never be the same for me since Ryan has died but I have decided it is going to be the best it can be despite Ryan's death and perhaps because of it. I truly hope I can honour him in a variety of ways including sharing how I have dealt with him no longer being a part of my life.

I truly believe my life will never be the same.

I have read about and tried other therapies. They include: yoga, massage therapy, aroma therapy, astrology, hypnotherapy, the pendulum, automatic writing, healing with gemstones and crystals. I will be looking further into some of these areas in the future when the time feels right for me. They are just on hold for now. I have to say that hypnotherapy intrigues me a lot, particularly when it deals with past lives for healing purposes. Even if I could use hypnotherapy to help friends and family with their phobias, it would be worth it.

The Pendulum

If you know anything about the ouiji board, you know something of the capability of the pendulum. A pendulum is a crystal on a short chain so it can be suspended to allow it to make circular motions or back and forth movements generally. You can make a crude version of one with a thread and needle and piece of jewelry. As long as it can swing freely it will work. Some people purchase special stones from Arizona or other places where there are vortexes of energy. I bought one in my favorite new age store in Almonte while shopping with one of my nieces, Lisa, who is my God-daughter. She is also into the spirits, angels, gem healing, Reiki and the pendulum, so of course it is fun to shop and compare notes with her. On one occasion, we went to her home, lit a candle and practiced using the pendulum. Lisa seemed more successful than me initially because she had already been using the pendulum. How do you know if you are successful? Well, if it moved at all, we got excited. But this is how it works. First you rub the pendulum between your fingers and blow a gentle breath on it. Ask the pendulum to show you "yes". Then, ask it to show you "no". Sometimes it goes clockwise and counterclockwise or it can go up and down and then sideways. There is no right way for you. To test the accuracy of the pendulum or if you are doing it right, you ask it questions that you already know the answers to. For example, ask it your age or how many children in your family. Always ask it a yes or no question. Then, you bravely ask it other questions for which you want the answer. It was a matter of waiting to see if the pendulum was right. After two and a half years I have also been doing automatic writing on a daily basis, followed by practicing the pendulum and recording the results. At the beginning of each session I would light a candle and invoke my spirits and guides to join me as well as my deceased relatives, especially Ryan. I asked each spirit if they were present and usually the answer was yes. The spirits like to be called upon because they like your attention and they like to help you. In doing, they are honouring God. I am only practicing the pendulum for my own use and enjoyment. I have come to the point that I can determine the outcome by my will. I seem to be controlling the pendulum. That is not the same as manipulating the pendulum to do what I want it to do. I need to learn to distract my thoughts allowing the pendulum to be guided by my guides. At this point I am not sure if the pendulum will be one of my tools in the future. Although, it is useful in association with Reiki to let you know if the chakras (the energy centers of your body) are blocked.

Automatic Writing

I thought when I came across **"automatic writing"** that it sounded so easy. You just sit there and allow the spirits to move the pen and put these thoughts on paper. After trying it for a couple of weeks without any success, I had seen a psychic medium in Winter Haven in Florida who said just write your thoughts down like journaling and just write whatever comes to your mind. Sometimes it is just about the kind of day I have had. From doing "angel cards', I have learned that this is how the angels and spirit guides communicate with us. They infuse thoughts and suggestions into our daily thinking. I thought my thoughts were my own but maybe not. The writing is much easier and I can discern which thoughts are my own and some that came from out there. You know, sometimes you say, I don't know where that idea came from.

Please note: When I went to see that psychic in Florida, she told me that Ryan told her that I write in a blue book and that I light a candle before I start to write. Both are true. Actually the book I wrote in at the time is one that I found in

Ryan's old bedroom after he passed away. For some reason I imagined that he would know that too. She also said that he wanted to tell me that when I write, HE IS THERE! You can bet I made sure that I made an entry each evening counting on the fact that he would be there.

You can ask the spirits questions when you are doing automatic writing, so I decided to give it a try. I asked Ryan if he would be one of my guides. The answer came immediately and loud as if he was shouting at me.

The answer I got was, "I ALREADY AM". I KNEW that was Ryan talking to me. They say sometimes you just know. I will continue the automatic writing because I do feel that Ryan is with me when I am doing it. Besides he told me he was there when I write. I feel like he is guiding me in my writing.

Meditation

I often tried **meditation** on my own after reading numerous chapters on the benefits of meditation. Like many other people I had a lot of trouble quieting my mind. Often many thoughts and ideas seeped into my mind interrupting the quiet. The next time I was in "Soul Scents", my store in Almonte, I noticed a flyer for a workshop on meditation. Since I was already in town and the session was that very evening I signed up. She had us practicing **deep breathing** and staring at a candle set in the middle of the floor as methods of meditation. But it wasn't until she put on a guided meditation tape that she had produced that I felt that I had reached that peaceful state. While being guided to a quiet place the soothing words allowed my brain to stay focused and remain calm, relaxed and positively inspired. That day, I had already purchased a meditation CD by Sonia Choquette with whom I am already familiar since I had just complete her book, **"Ask Your Guides"** and I already own and enjoy her Angel cards to match. It has been an amazing CD to use and I finally feel that I have successfully been able to meditate. Sonia's CD gives three guided meditations as follows: Getting Ready for Meditation, Opening your Heart and Connecting to Divine Source and Energizing Your Body to Raise Your Vibration. This is followed be appropriate music selections to aid you in meditating without the guidance. I will, however, try from time to time to do it on my own. I have learned from her that it is important to practice deep breathing to prepare for the meditative state. To do deep breathing effectively I was taught to take a deep breath through your nose to the count of four. Hold that breath for the count of four. Then, breathe out through your mouth. It is an important form of detoxing the body. Who knew? Everyone should take the time to do deep breathing every day. As a matter of fact it should be done throughout the day to feed oxygen to the brain and give you a quiet and energizing break. You can do it anytime or anywhere. We all have to breathe anyway. You may as well do it to benefit your body more effectively. Try it now! Everyone could use the breaks in our daily lives to stop and give our bodies and our brains a well needed rest through the deep breathing. It is also a good way to de-stress. You can take a better break once you are at home and give yourself some privacy to meditate. Some people like to do it when they go to bed at night or when they wake up in the morning to start their day in a peaceful way. I enjoy bedtime and then I just drift off for the night.

Angels

Everyone likes **angels**. Even people who no longer go to Church or believe in God like angels. Do you know how many kinds of angels there are? Do you know that they will give assistance any time? You just have to ask! Their job is to help you and by so doing they are honoring God. Let me tell you about them. The word angel means "messenger". They deliver Heaven's love and guidance. Everyone has their own Guardian Angel(s) that they have had from the time they were born. Sometimes people have more than one. They are with you for life watching over you whether you know it or not or whether you talk to them or not. Other angels will come and go throughout your life depending on your needs. They are like specialists; they are there to help you with different and more complicated situations. Angels are non-denominational and help people of different faiths or no faith. You can always call on the angels for all things big and small.

There are nine choirs of angels from the highest order down: Seraphim, Cherubim, Thrones, Dominions, Virtues,

Powers, Principalities and Archangels. Each level has its own specialty. The highest level is closer to God. And the lowest level is closer to humanity. There are countless other angels too. There are angels for about any need you can think of. There are healing angels, romantic angels, fitness angels, angels of abundance, family angels, etc. and you can call on them to assist in any situation. Guardian Angels and Archangels are mostly involved in helping humanity and the earth. There are even many kinds of Archangels with their own specialties. For example, Archangel Michael is called on for power and protection. Archangel Gabriel is in charge of communication. Archangel Raphael assists in healing. You can talk to the angels aloud or in your thoughts and ask them for help and then wait for a sign. These will be thoughts, feelings or impressions, words or pictures. They may leave small white feathers or coins to let you know they are near. It may be a sign on a billboard or a song on the radio that may give you a clue to help solve your problem. If you hear, see or think a message three times it is a sign for sure. Of course you should not forget to thank your angels for their help. If you don't, they will think you do not appreciate their help. They like to be acknowledged. I wouldn't even think of leaving my driveway without asking for their protection for a safe trip even if I am only going the short five kilometer trip to town for groceries. The prayer I say now is: "May the light of the Holy Spirit protect me on my journey today. Angels and archangels protect me. Ryan, please be with me. I love you. I miss you; 'til we meet again." Did you notice I called on the Holy Spirit? He is the greatest spirit of all. You may as well call on the best. You don't need to use my words; you can compose one yourself that will be just as good.

I remember one day I was approaching a 50km speed limit and I heard a (thought) message to slow down. I thought that particular place was a stupid place to require us to slow down to 50 km so I continued on going at 80 km. Sure enough I met a police cruiser and got a speeding ticket. As I was driving away I said aloud, "I know, I know, you told me to slow down." You do get messages if you are open to them. Sometimes they are just my own thoughts but I am not so sure anymore whether they are mine or messages from my angels. I am much more careful now particularly at that same spot. How arrogant of me to think all my thoughts are my own. Sometimes I know they are messages from angels, spirit guides or deceased loved ones that are trying to help or protect me. Now, if I get a string of green lights when I am in a hurry, I remember to say thank you to whoever made that happen for me. It may sound a little like I am losing it but it is a really nice way of thinking of things and can you prove it wasn't help from the other side?

Angel Cards

Since I have acquired an interest in angels and I now have my own special angel, Ryan, in Heaven, it was a natural step in my progression to try angel cards. Each time I visited the ladies who gave Reiki treatments and the psychics who gave me readings I was given the opportunity to choose an angel card. This card would give me some direction in my life that was germane at that time. It was uncanny how many times the message was meaningful to me that day. So on my next trip to Soul Scents I picked up a deck, read the easy instructions and started to do my own angel cards on a daily basis. Let me tell you how easy it is. You need to shuffle the cards to put your energy into the deck. You select an aspect of your life that you would like an answer to or ideas to follow. Then select a card, or three or seven. These are called a spread. Some cards have a message on them; often you must look up the meaning in the little book that accompanies the deck for further meaning. I like to shuffle the deck until three cards 'pop out'. I feel that the angels have selected them that way instead of just picking out three cards. But suit yourself. A lot of your own intuition is used to determine the meaning of the cards. The same three cards could mean something somewhat different if it is in reference to a different situation or a different person. Most of the cards are positive and are both encouraging and supportive. Some of the cards though tell you that you need to develop better skills in patience, compromise, exercise for example. If the same cards surface repeatedly, then they are letting you know that you need to continue to work in that area or give you encouragement that you are going to reach your goal. My all-time favorite card is from the angel Sonya. She gives me a message from my deceased loved one, (in my mind Ryan) and tells me that he is happy, at peace, loves me very much and I should not worry about him. I look forward to getting this very special message. Another card called confidence suggests you don't need to have confidence in yourself that you only need confidence in God.

As well as using the angel cards, I now find that I pray to the angels and ask for assistance much more often for everything from protection to keeping the traffic light green until I drive through it. You would be surprised how often this works. You can ask for protection from negativity if you have to spend some time with someone you know will drag you down. Perhaps they were in a bad mood or just being negative that day. If you forget to ask the angels beforehand, you can ask to remove the negativity from your body after the fact. You can find these angel cards in the larger bookstores. They are usually in the same isle as the books on angels. That is sometimes called the New Age or Metaphysical section. There are a number of these decks and you should buy the one that speaks to you on that particular day. Consider that guidance from your guardian angel or your spirit guides. They love to help and be thanked. Pick the ones that appeals to you through the words, colours or the artwork on them. That will be the right one for you that day. That's your intuition working for you or your angels giving you guidance.

Family

Most people are uncomfortable talking about the death of a loved one. When you are the one with the loss, you can recognize that look of fear on their faces as an indicator of their discomfort. Often they do not know what to say, but let me tell you, they don't need to say anything. Just let the one suffering the loss to say what they need or want to say. From experience, the one you have lost is always on your mind. I think of Ryan constantly because so many things remind me of him. My husband, Bob and my sisters and my brother allow me to refer to Ryan in our everyday conversations. I have no intention of ever forgetting Ryan, so he will be as much a part of my life as if he were still alive. Here are many things that are constant reminders of him such as pictures around the house, tulips (because we walked through the Tulip Festival in Ottawa when he was really sick), dragonflies of course since they are his sign for me, blankets I used to brighten up the hospital room that I now use while watching TV or in the car (It is like a hug from him because he used it.), the LOWE name for the hardware store, the Apple logo or the rl logo for Ralph Lauren products. There is a really long list and new ones surprise me from time to time. You will find different things remind you of your loved one that will be entirely different from mine, but they are there. The question is will you share them with others or will you suffer all by yourself? I think it is necessary to get talking about illness and death because I believe it helps the healing process so you can eventually get on with your life. That is the best way to honour your family member or friend who passed away. It does get easier with time and it is now easier to talk to my siblings about their personal situations and plan for their final wishes. They should let their children know now rather than deal with death and the funeral arrangements at the time when it is so emotional and difficult to think straight. You never know when your time will come. It is not just the elderly that die.

My husband, Bob, is my best friend and my soul mate. He was my "rock" through Ryan's illness, death and afterwards.

My husband, Bob, has been my rock through Ryan's illness and death. They say the loss of a child can ruin a marriage. But in my case, Bob helped pull me through the dark days. When Ryan was severely ill and I was going to Ottawa on an almost daily basis, he would take the phone calls for me and update people on Ryan's condition. I was living it and I did not have the stamina to talk about it too when I returned home at night. I did appreciate their calls though and their support. After Ryan died, he did a lot of listening and we did a lot of talking. I recall the day that he said to me, "I don't want to lose you over this." I knew what he meant. He was afraid that I would go into a deep depression and not be able to dig my way out of it. It was one more reason I had to work harder at getting better. He had nothing to fear; I had no intention of dealing with grief in this way. So I turned to him and said, "you won't lose me dear because I have you." I quickly buried myself in reading books looking for answers. I would tell him what each book was about and he would tell me what he agreed with or not. I got into some pretty heavy subjects such as whether there was an afterlife, reincarnation and past lives. It opened up a whole new world for us. I am the explorer and he is the sounding board. I don't know if he knew what he was getting in for but he does realize that I am on some kind of journey and he is in the backseat coming along for the ride. The one thing that impressed me the most is that he has started to accompany me to Church. I did not ask him to or expect him to do it; he just did. I just think it was his way of being supportive. Thank you, Bob.

I Want to Move

It has been a desire for me to move back to Almonte since I retired in 2000 because my entire family is there. My main reason is to be closer to my three sisters and my brother in order to spend more time with them since they are older than I am. While I worked my entire career before 2000 I did not see them that much. I would be making up for time lost. My main obstacle is that Bob does not want to leave Renfrew and our present home on forty four acres in the country because he loves the privacy and it is the house he has lived in the longest in his entire life.

Unfortunately I have this continual pull to be in Almonte. I have been lucky enough to nurture a relationship with my nieces and great nieces to date and I would love that connection to grow in the future. It has been fun being Aunt Judy particularly since I am now gaining some great nieces and even great-great nieces and nephews. Boy, am I getting up there. They don't replace my son Ryan but they do give me some others to get to know and spend time with and perhaps help out in some way.

We have had a number of couples look at the house but only one offer to date and he could not get the money he needed. So Bob is getting his wish of staying in the house and I am struggling with learning patience. Another thought we have had is that perhaps Ryan is blocking the sale of the house since he probably wants us to stay near Jon and Lyndsey. One of my psychics told me that Ryan really liked our house because that was where he lived when he went to high school. So who knows? For some reason we are still there. I often get an angel card that is called "Blessing in Disguise" and I am wondering if that is the blessing; we are meant to stay put. Jon still lives in Renfrew and he and Lyndsey will probably raise their family there because her extended family is there too. I definitely won't want to be too far away when I start to have grandchildren of my own.

What we have done in the meantime is to put our trailer at a park just fifteen minutes from Almonte and if I want or need to be in Almonte for a couple of days I use the trailer as an apartment. It is a lovely recreational spot with a pool and a man-made lake. It is a compromise for the time being. I can also stay with my oldest sister, Benita, any time I want but the trailer works best for when Bob is with me. The park is also equidistant from the airport, where Bob spends a lot of time, as the airport is from our home so he is at no inconvenience.

The dragonfly is about 40 inches long and wide. It is on our double car garage next to our home in Renfrew. It is one of the first things people notice when they drive up our driveway. This is another way to always remember Ryan.

Hobbies

Before Ryan passed away, my favourite pastime was quilting. It is something I have in common with all three of my sisters. To date I have not returned to quilting; I just lost interest in it. Instead I have been reading feverishly to gain knowledge, interest and insight on death and the afterlife. My second favourite hobby has evolved in time (and improved I might add) since taking it up again. I knew I had to get involved in something after Ryan died and I offered to play the piano for the choir at the Renfrew Manor every Wednesday for my friend, Colleen, for the six months that we are at home in Renfrew. Then when we go to Florida I play for the group called the Harmoniers in Woodbrook Park where we live. We practice every Wednesday morning and go to a different seniors' home each week. It is very rewarding to be part of that group. I now am the leader; so I pick out the music, copy the words for the songs as well as play for the performances. The seniors are such an appreciative audience; they are enjoying the fact that we would spend the time and energy to visit them. Sometimes, we are told, we are their only visitors; that is so sad. The more I practiced, I better I got. I was feeling needed and accomplishing some improvement in my God given talent. I never thought I was particularly good, just willing. The seniors seem to enjoy the music. My point here is that you need to find a reason to get up in the morning and have a real purpose. It is difficult to be stuck in your grief when you are bringing joy to someone else.

Once I was home again, I was asked to play music in the chronic care wing of the hospital in Almonte. I used the various programs that I had prepared for my group in Florida. I did that twice a month for a sing-a-long. I bring copies of the words so patients can sing too. My sister, Benita, also asked me to play at the nursing home where her husband, Art, was admitted. I said yes, as long as she would help lead the singing. Later I thought I may as well ask the other nursing home in Almonte if they would like some time for singing and they promptly signed me up for twice a month too. This is no additional work for me because I use the same programs that I developed over the years for my Florida group. The words are all on computer and I make enough copies for the larger groups, fifty in number. I swear I get as much out of these sessions as they do, maybe more. As I said to you, it is difficult to be stuck in your grief when you are bringing joy to someone else. Often when the session is finished, some of the patients or clients will thank me for coming and sharing my time with them or they would say that they really enjoyed the music.

I have discovered that music is an amazing tool for seniors. My program is about twenty songs long. About eight songs are from the 20's, 30's or 40's, about eight songs are from the 50's and 60's and the last four would be hymns or gospel music. After that part of the program I play only the melody for some songs and ask them to "name that tune". Sometime they get it and sometimes they don't but if I start to sing the words their memory seems to be jogged and they start singing. They seem to have such pride if they do recall the title of the song. I call it music therapy.

This is my new "pool' garden. Oddly enough I created an Indian medicine wheel in it. Was I native Indian in another life? The deer have not found out it is there yet. Yeh!

I guess I have always had one more hobby. I like to garden. I used to spend a lot of time as a child helping Dad with the gardening, both flowers and the vegetable garden. I have flower gardens in both locations where we live and I plant a garden for Louise in Florida. She is a ninety-three year old soul who lives next door to us. She is partially blind and unable to attend to her garden. I also plant a vegetable garden in Renfrew. As a child I always gardened with my Father and the interest just stuck. Besides I love the fresh produce at harvest time when you get to taste and appreciate the fruits of your labour. I never really thought of it as work. It is a time to be closer to nature and soothe your soul. It is a very enjoyable time of meditation. At home in Renfrew when the novelty of the above ground pool wore off and the boys left home, I decided to make it a garden. In my previous location the deer often got the bounty before I did. So, we got a truck load of top soil and Jon spread it all around inside the pool as well as ten bags of mushroom compost. I planted the garden and the deer are no wiser. It has been the most productive garden since I have relocated it to the pool. I now climb down the ladder to work in my garden. I thought it would be a good idea to lay boards down in the garden from twelve o'clock to six o'clock and from nine o'clock to three o'clock in order to keep my feet from getting too dirty from the soil. I made the space in the very center larger by using two bricks inside each corner. Without realizing it I had made an Indian medicine wheel in my garden. Where did that come from? I am convinced that I must have been native Indian in another life. This is another idea I got from some of my readings as well as part of a conversation with Heather. We tend to see hints of a previous life in our present surroundings. I find my time in the garden very relaxing and therapeutic. One has a lot of time to think while gardening. I often think of my Dad and all the time I spent gardening with him. Of course I think of Ryan too. That is a given.

Psychic Mediums

NOW, THIS IS THE TOPIC I THINK YOU ARE GOING TO ENJOY THE MOST. I certainly enjoyed my time spent talking to the people who can talk to your deceased love ones. I have been interested in these people over the years. I have been to fortune tellers, tea leaf readers and the occasional psychic as well as tarot card readers. But my interest blossomed after Ryan passed because I needed a link to him even if it was through a middle person. I learned from my reading that you do not always get to talk to the person you want; the spirit that appears will be the one who wants to talk to you. There is a couple of TV shows that reveal how that works such as Long Island Psychic and John Edwards. First the psychic will tell you things about you or your loved one that convinces you that he or she really is talking to a particular spirit by telling you something that he or she could not possibly know otherwise. Then when they give you a message from your loved one you believe what they have to say. I know, I know. It is also what you want to hear. But as you go on, you wonder how the heck they can come up with this information unless the psychic IS talking to your loved one.

Over the first year that Ryan was departed, I saw four psychics and a tarot card reader. I met with Laura, Jewels, Angela and Blair (in a public performance) and Donna, a tarot card practitioner and a tea leaf reader. Yes, it may seem that I was desperate and I was. I was desperate to have some kind of link to Ryan now that he was gone and I found a way to have that link. I also got some information from Heather, who did my Reiki treatments and training. I coveted each morsel of information that each of these persons gave me. It was like putting a puzzle together with each person mentioned above offering the puzzle pieces. Sometimes I figured out a piece by myself. For example when I was practicing automatic writing and I asked Ryan directly if he would be one of my very own spirit guides, I heard immediately, "I already am". That was comforting to know that he had taken up that role for me from the Other Side. I also learned a lot from watching "Ghost Whisperer" on television. It gave a very good indication of passing through the white light and talking to spirits. I received a lot of valuable information from these people about Ryan which was my only goal initially. But I also got information about me, my other two sons, Bob and Ryan's biological father. I will only share the information about Ryan and me for privacy of information reasons. Perhaps you will see how the pieces form a real picture as I relay some of the information. Suffice is it to say that each tidbit of information was VERY meaningful to me. The information was my link to Ryan for the time being. Sometimes I was allowed to ask Ryan a question and I got a response from him (through the psychic, of course). It was like talking to him through an interpreter. I am going to present the information in chronological order so you get the information as I received it.

You can decide for yourself if this is something you would consider doing after you hear the kinds of things I learned. I have to tell you I have two sisters that think I have lost it and one does not think I am dealing with the loss of Ryan very well. My view is that I have gained so much information and it is helping me heal and deal with the grief. Everyone is different and this is my way. One of my sisters asked me if it was scary. My answer to her was that it was not scary to me but it was very exciting and that one day I hope to be able to communicate with Ryan on my own. I am still working on that. You will see the differences between the psychics and in how much information they shared with me and the kind of information they shared. I valued each of them for their contribution.

> One day I hope to be able to
> communicate with Ryan on my own.

Laura Traplin   *Aug 8, 2011*

Laura was the first person I went to see. My niece, Lisa, had been to see her and was totally amazed with the information that she shared with her and the accuracy of the things she said to Lisa. Since she is my niece I know of these people too and the information given. I was so impressed that I immediately booked an appointment hoping that I would hear from Ryan. I knew there were no guarantees but I would probably hear from one of my deceased relatives and perhaps they could give me some information about Ryan. Heather, a Shamanic practitioner, also recommended Laura to me. Let me tell you that Laura was absolutely amazing! She connected me to my Maternal Grandmother, my Mother, my Father and Ryan all on my first visit. I wasn't really thinking about my other relatives but it was so comforting. It opened up a whole new chapter for me in my search for information to my journey in life. Allow me to share some tidbits from this visit. The information may seem a little scattered. It does not always flow to make the most sense but the pieces do make sense and they can be strung together upon contemplation. Laura's words will be preceded by her initials and my initials will precede my thoughts. I had never talked to Laura before my appointment and the first thing she said to me when I arrived was not to tell her anything.

LT   His hair has changed. It is now shorter and lighter. He said he was hit on the head; he doesn't understand what happened. He said, "You just go along minding your own business and it comes back and bites you on the behind." His energy is pure. He is wonderful and very loving. He was good to everyone. He was always that friend that made you laugh. He said his head hurt; there was a lot of pressure in his head and he said he could not swallow. I don't get the impression that he was ever irresponsible; he was just a good honest kid. He had a diagnosis, yes? He was not happy about it at all. He was very angry about it for three months. He could not come to terms with it all as to why his life would be cut shorter than others. He said that is not what I agreed to (in his chart on the other Side) before he was born.

JS   This first bit confirms that he told her about his diagnosis of cancer and the exact pain that he was tolerating through his illness. The reference to the chart confirmed for me the information I read about that we each make our own life chart before we are born. We select our family, our career and our time of death among other things. Why he picked thirty-one years of age to die I will not know until I am on the Other Side too.

LT   There is a very big bond between the two of you. It is huge and over many lifetimes. Ryan said he was mad at you when he was about fourteen because you always knew everything. He wanted to vomit a lot when he was younger; he had a very sick stomach. He said you would fuss over him and you always knew what was better. He said he could not communicate the last two weeks he was alive and he heard what you were saying to him. You were brave. He loved all the flowers at the service—beautiful YELLOW flowers. (He laughed).

JS Indeed, he could no longer talk the last two weeks because his vocal chords were paralyzed. The flowers were mostly red roses, both on his casket and a bouquet from his brothers that Jon and Lyndsey chose. He laughed because he was just showing us he had a sense of humour that they were yellow.

LT He is singing a Rolling Stones song, "You can't always get what you want." He is very wise and intuitive. He did come to terms with things in the last month. He said he was okay. Ryan said his back was hurting.

 Now he is sucking on ice cubes to keep his lips wet. He said, "At this point, it was just about orgasmic!" Laura remarked on his sense of humour. He wants you to write that book. It is about bereavement and grieving Mothers. It is more than that. It is about life and death and the hardships they go through and they still find the grace to continue.

JS Derek and I used to give Ryan a wet sponge on a stick like a lollipop to keep his lips wet and to get a drink in his final days. He would suck on it. I am writing that book.

LT Do you remember that he used to walk in the door and yell "hey-ho? I don't have to tell you how much he loved you. He depended on you (Mom) in particular from the age of seven. He knows that when you get into bed at night, that the sheets have to be cool and crisp, not bunched up and that HE IS WITH YOU.

JS   Ryan used to yell "YO" when he came in the door announcing his arrival. I would yell "yo" back to him. At bedtime, I would go upstairs when Bob was retiring and turn down the sheets on my side and go back downstairs for another hour or so. It is nice to know that he is with me. It makes you think he sees and knows everything. Do you believe that?

      Well, that was my first visit to a psychic since Ryan's passing. I got a lot of other information for other people too but I am not sharing that here. What a lot of confirming information. What a lot of personal messages from Ryan to me. It was very heartwarming to hear all of that. No one told Laura any information. I had never met her before. There is NO WAY that she could know the things beforehand that she shared about Ryan's struggle with cancer. So, of course I chose to believe the other stuff she shared with me that Ryan told her. One visit and I now believe that psychics CAN talk to the dead and relay important messages to loved ones here on earth. I will seek out others too. Make sure you find one that is reputable.

Blair Robertson   *Oct. 4, 2011*

On Tuesday, October 4th, 2011 Blair Robertson, who is a psychic medium, gave a performance and group reading at the Civitan Hall in Almonte. One of my nieces, Meaghan, works at a shop called Blackbirds and they were sponsoring it.

She called to see if I would be interested in attending. Well, is the sky blue? Of course I did.

It would give me an opportunity to see a live reading of someone else in the audience. After he gave a reading to a couple of other persons in the hall, he moved near to where I was sitting. He began giving a few clues to see if it rang true for anyone in my area. They seemed familiar to me but it was not clear to me that the message was for me. I did not expect that it would be. After all, what are the chances? A lady behind me was certain that the message was for her anyway. As he continued the reading, she became less sure it was for her and it started to peak my interest. The last clue convinced me, without a doubt, that Ryan had come through to me. I did not want to reveal that fact in public because of what the audience might think of me for not recognizing that fact until the last clue. Blair moved on to another spirit. These were the clues he gave and you will see that they could easily have been for a number of people in the audience initially: father or father figure, he had a badge like a fireman, sick for a long time, he was in a coma when he passed away, someone named John was close to him (this clue caught my attention), you held his hand at the time when he passed, and someone didn't make it for the passing. Let me explain. My husband, Bob, is Ryan's stepdad. He did have an honorary police badge given to him by the Chief of police for all his work in collaboration with them in his last school board in York Region which is just north of Toronto. Jon is his younger brother. I did hold his hand for hours on end in the last number of days. Finally, Bob had been travelling back and forth from Renfrew in the last week while I stayed there for the week and he was about an hour late the day of his passing. Every clue was bang on but it wasn't until the last couple of clues that I KNEW it was indeed Ryan for me. What a thrill to think that Ryan would come through to me in a public forum. There was no way that Blair had any knowledge of me nor could he have known the intimate details of Ryan's death. Can you see why I was beginning to believe that these psychics had a real gift and it was a vehicle for me to be in touch with Ryan? After his performance I purchased another pendulum and his DVD on how to develop you own intuition. I still have not viewed this. As of yet, the package is still unopened. I guess the timing is not yet right for me to venture into this area. Sometime in the future I will take this on.

Donna Kinniburg   *Oct. 11, 2011*

I continued my search and decided to try a tarot card reader in Renfrew. She works out of the local health food store in Renfrew on Thursdays only. I found out she also reads tea leaves. Of course I went there hoping to connect with Ryan. I knew that may not happen and that I may well hear from another relative from the past. Donna shared a new bit of information to me which helped me along on the healing process. Now Donna has a different method of sharing information. She asks questions and I know what you are thinking. You are thinking that I am giving her information. But, I would explain that Donna develops the information in her own unique way. I will include some explanations indicated by my initials. Let us begin.

DK Who is the Capricorn?

JS My son, Ryan.

DK What is your relationship?

JS Somewhat aloof.

DK Capricorns are like that. Capricorn has passed, yes? He was your Father in another life. He is still around you now. So, when he is around, it is your son AND your Father from another life. In another life when your father died, you were so upset that you attempted suicide. Your son decided to be more distant this time so you would not have such a strong connection this time.

JS I don't know that she is correct in how upset I would be with Ryan's passing. I don't know of any greater hurt in my life. I have lost both of my parents, but in comparison, my loss of Ryan was much deeper.

DK How old was your son?

JS Thirty-one.

DK That is why the whole family was in a state of confusion. The grief period starts with the diagnosis, so you had many years of struggling. You are going to get a message from your spirit guides and he will be part of it. The message comes in the form of a question and it is something you want to ask yourself.

Donna indicated two decks of cards on the table explaining that one deck is of light hearted questions and the second deck held deeper issues. Being very excited about connecting to the spirit world, I chose a card from the deeper issues. The card I chose asked the following question: "If you wrote a book today, what would be the title? Donna said she had goose bumps. I have read that this indicates the spirit is present. She said you are writing a book about him, eh? Are you going to add things like life is not over? TO LET ANYONE ELSE KNOW WOULD BE HEALING FOR THEM TOO. He is encouraging you to continue with this.

JS   When I chose that card, I threw it on the table and laughed. She looked at me curiously. I said I already named my book and I had a pseudo book cover made for it. I shared the title with her. Well, the book had been started but I was working at it sporadically. I thought I guess I better get at it more seriously. Ryan was telling me to go for it.

Jewels   *Oct. 27, 2011*

Jewels was the name of an interesting English lady, I believe. She was doing reading in the back of the shop I mentioned earlier in Almonte, the Blackbird. My niece, Meaghan works there part time and asked me if I would like an appointment. Yes, I was interested in acquiring more information about Ryan in particular and I would like to support the shop for having this kind of service right in Almonte. I was also pleased that Meaghan thought of me. I also did a follow-up meeting at Jewels' home which included tea leaf reading and choosing angel cards. Again, I was still collecting those puzzle pieces to help me understand why Ryan was taken from us so young and get some help on how to survive without him and get more information about the hereafter. Here is what transpired:

J   There is a young man healing in spirit and healing his body. His name is Brian or Ryan. He is with Pappy or Poppy. Your Mom and Dad are also with him. He was in transition for quite a while, but he is fine now. He was in your house frequently in the early days after he passed. He regrets that he was so closed in to himself. He was a Capricorn and a hard worker. His sickness took over his body. He loved Christmas at home; it was special to him.

JS   Ryan IS his name and his grandfather's name on his dad's side was "Pappy". These two pieces of information confirm that she is indeed a psychic medium too. I have read that it takes time for spirits to heal too. This reading was almost two years after his passing and it does feel good to picture him again as whole and not ravaged by cancer. He definitely was a hard worker. He had a great work ethic. He used to say when he took a phone call or went to the bathroom when he was working, he would add time to the client for whom he was working. Christmas was always a very special time for me too and the rest of the family because it was really the only time we were all together.

J   Ryan is carving now. He has children with him. They are laughing. He teases them and jokes with them. They love him. Ryan said that you should not fear your healing power; it is your destiny. He continued by saying, "As you do so, you transfer your own suffering from the loss of him and other lifetimes to compassion and love."

JS   It is nice to hear that he is working with children. He wanted to get married and have a family before he was taken from us. I guess this is his new family on the Other Side. I appreciate Ryan's encouragement to continue my healing work which I started in order to heal from my own grief. The Reiki has been a gift for me and one I can now share with others. My book has been a very healing process too which just started out as a journal for my own use. At a certain point I realized that perhaps the information could be helpful to others going through the same ordeal. So, here we are. I hope it is helpful for you. You could write a journal. It is a great release of emotion and something you can choose to share or not. Can you see how more of the pieces are coming together for me in my puzzle? It is certainly coming together for me and is most helpful and encouraging to me each time I receive more tidbits of information about Ryan.

Heather Brown

I don't really have only one specific date for Heather since we have met many times for Reiki treatments, Women's Journeys and Reiki training sessions. I had been going to another lady for Reiki and my niece Lisa told me she had been to see Heather and had really benefitted from her sessions and felt really relaxed afterwards. She encouraged me to try her for a session. Besides, she lives in Almonte and I am there often. Thankfully I did. We connected right away. She is so warm and upbeat. Over my times with Heather she also has shared some interesting information about Ryan. She too said that Ryan was well and at peace on the Other Side. She said he is with someone we know (she was his babysitter when he was a toddler) who also died of cancer and together they are welcoming children and helping them to cross over to the Other Side. I chose to believe this information to be true. I have read that spirits do have particular tasks to do when they get there to help others. I have shared experiences with other ladies who are also Reiki Masters and enjoy partaking in a group of like-minded people. In her Womens' Journeys we release things from our past and forgive people for their transgressions in order to help with our personal healing. It is interesting that a number of the people in the group have suffered some personal loss or anguish and are searching for some assistance too as well as helping others. Thank you, Heather in helping me on my journey. Heather is a shamanic practitioner and a Reiki Master and teacher. What a gift she has for helping others. Did I mention that I taught Heather in kindergarten in Pakenham? I did not know before I went that she was from my past. I recognized her eyes and her beautiful smile. As well, her laugh is infectious. I am really glad that our lives have crossed paths once again. She is very encouraging and challenges clients to share their gifts. On our last visit, she challenged me to take part in a workshop coming up in the spring at the Mill of Kintail just outside Almonte. Heather, I am working on it. I am sure I will be there.

Gay H. Feb. 12, 2012

I have mentioned the term synchronicity earlier in this book. It is the amazing coincidence of meeting people or happenings in a particular timeframe or order. I have heard from a couple of sources that I should write a book. Well, I learned that there was a lady in the park in Florida where we live in the winter months who does self-publishing and helps people write a book. Myrna, at our Ladies' Auxiliary meeting suggested that perhaps we should invite her to one our meetings but we just never got around to it. That is how I first heard about her. My sister, Mary, comes down to the park for the months of February and March with her husband, Greg. On one particular day, Gay walked by their place and had a chat with both Mary and Greg. They told me that she lived kitty-corner to them. Putting two and two together I knew this was the lady I wanted to get to know. This is where I got the nagging idea that indeed I should write a book. On one of my visits to Laura, I remembered that I told her that I thought I would like to write and a book and she said that Ryan just interrupted and said, "Why don't you?" With that in mind I got up my nerve and knocked on her door and introduced myself to her. She was a delightful person to meet.

After sharing a part of my story with her, she loaned me copies of two manuscripts that she was working on and a book that she used when she taught her workshop. There were some very helpful suggestions to get me moving along the way. When I was there she also invited me to a workshop in Winter Haven on how to manifest what you want. While I was there I found out that the lady who was presenting the workshop is also a medium. You know very well what that meant. I booked an appointment and made my way over to Winter Haven to an appointment with her. I secretly told myself that I would work on my book over the six months back at home and have it ready for Gay's perusal in the fall when I came back.

While at the course with Gay we created vision boards which are large pieces of Bristol board on which we glue pictures and words cut from magazines which portray our desires for your future. I had just finished reading the book and watching the DVD for "The Secret" which tells you to do exactly the same thing. More synchronicity was happening. Gay had not read the book so I loaned it to her with the DVD. There was some synchronicity for her too.

Angela Hewitt   *April 7, 2112*

I couldn't help noticing that in her first name was the word "angel". As usual I went with my paper and pencil to record what she had to say. It was a good job that I did because she did not record the session as the others had. She began by saying:

AH Ryan is giving you permission to live. A white feather is a sign from him. He said when you are writing in the blue book HE IS THERE! You light a candle when you do this. He is taking credit for your writing. She said he is handsome, flirtatious and charming. He said you bought a sun hat; it is tan, with a band around it. He said it is silly!

JS I **do** write in a blue book. As a matter of fact it was a book left over when he left home. I found it in his room after he died. I **do** light a candle when I write. I **did** buy a tan hat with a band around it to keep the sun off my face. He would say it was silly. Actually he would say I looked silly. What mother would not want to hear the compliments for one of her children?

AH Ryan said he is around for the everyday stuff. **I am to write about communicating with Ryan.** He said "don't worry about it. You will get there. Help others." She said he sits next to me. He is my buddy. He also said, "tell my brother that I am happy for him getting married and having a family. You have my blessing. Please keep on living. She is pretty. (He winks.) Good job! It wasn't meant for me in this lifetime." Angela said he was an old soul; he has lived many lives. Ryan said that when it is my time, he will be there.

JS This is another message that I am to write a book and he is taking credit for it. I'll give him that. Angela did not even know Ryan had a brother let alone that he was getting married. I had told her nothing. That was a nice message to his brother. It is nice to know that he will help me cross over when it is my turn. Thank goodness I had done all the reading I have done or a lot of what these psychics were telling me would not make a lot of sense. If you are considering going to a psychic medium, there is some basic reading available that would help you understand some of their references. I am not saying you have to do the reading but it certainly gave me a deeper understanding as I went along. You are able to ask both the psychic medium and the spirit who appeared at the session questions for clarification.

Pat Brown the Hypnotist

I went online to see if I could find a Reiki Master for a treatment while in Florida. While surfing the net, I found Pat Brown who was a Reiki Master and she also did hypnotism. That was on my list to try because that is how you get to your past lives. Now you must believe in reincarnation (on this earth) to get to this point. So, I phoned for an appointment. It was right there in Lakeland, Florida. I decided to try hypnosis to lose weight to see how it works. I could just have easily chosen my claustrophobia to work on. I ended up doing a four week program for weight loss and I have to report that it worked as long as I stayed on the program and listened to the taped sessions daily. At the time, I was surprised that I did not really feel that I was in a trance and that I could have gotten up and left at any time. She said that I was in control of myself at all times and I could have opened my eyes and left at any time. It was definitely not what I expected. Then on the last day, I asked her if she did **past life regression.** She said she did so I booked another appointment. Once again, I felt like I was in full control. She asked me a number of questions like what were my surroundings, what was I wearing, what was on my feet, etc. I felt like I was making up the answers at the time but I read that you would not be able to imagine something that you have not lived and experienced before (in a past life). When I visited Laura once again her method was very similar. I guess that process works. The jury is still out on the past lives theory. I may delve into hypnotherapy in the future again. It would be satisfying if I could help my friends and relatives with their various phobias.

Summer of 2012

We returned home at the end of April from our winter in Florida and I promptly booked another appointment with Laura Traplin. Unfortunately that would not be until September the 12th. I spent the summer working on my Reiki for myself and anyone else that would let me work on them. It is funny that my sisters are a little leery of the treatment but my nieces are willing participants. It makes me realize that the younger generation is searching; at least the females seem to be searching for information and treatments that are more holistic in nature and they are willing to talk about the hereafter. My goal was to get my Masters in Reiki. I wanted to reach that goal before returning to Florida. I did. At this time I do not see myself teaching it. Heather says yes. Who knows?

I also continued my **automatic writing** or journaling but this became sporadic because I started to concentrate more on the writing of my book. This started to take the bulk of my time. I continued to practice my **angel cards** almost daily. I found them to be most comforting and most encouraging for my new creative project. It was fun to do the angel cards for anyone who was willing to give them a try. Most of the time, the participants were amazed at how closely the cards spoke to their lives. I continued to perform my music at the Manor and the senior homes for the summer helping me pass the time until my next appointment with Laura. Gardening helped as well.

Laura Traplin   *Sept. 12, 2012*

This is a much longer session than before and very informative. Check out what she had to say this time. Remember that Laura has seen me before but it was over a year ago and she has had hundreds of readings since then.

LT   Your son is smart, very good looking and has a nice build. She said he could have an edge to him. He said to her that he didn't know what is better, his good looks, his smile or his brains.

JS   What mother would not want to hear these words? They are true. He did have an edge to him.

LT   He wants to apologize for the last seven months of his life. He said that you did not stop coming to visit him and do things for him but he was angry. He took a lot from you and did not give to you. He was angry at the situation and he knew he was being short, intolerant and demanding but he just couldn't help himself. He just could not believe what the outcome was going to be. At age twenty seven there was a shift in his body.

JS   He did not need to apologize to us. I would have been there through anything. Actually, I did not see him as intolerant or demanding. I saw him as being very brave and never complaining although I knew he was in extreme pain all the time. We could not believe what the outcome was going to be either.

LT   Laura said that all of a sudden she had no saliva in her mouth. Psychic mediums often feel the same symptoms as the spirit they are channeling. She said that she could not swallow and the pain in her head was extreme. She was experiencing Ryan's pain. He so much wanted to stay. He was angry that no one could fix him when they could fix so many things. Why couldn't they just pull it out of his head?

JS   One of Ryan's cancers was brain cancer. WE were angry that they could not fix him as well.

LT   That's how he was feeling while he was on earth. He realized the benefits, although limitations, of life on earth. Now he can see, now that he is on the Other

Side. He would get so frustrated with people because they did not have enough common sense. Some people would understand him. He sometimes had difficulty in relationships because he was abrupt. Other times he was so strong in his opinions. He admitted he wasn't very "frigging" flexible. He saw things in his life and in his education as very logical. He said, "Boy, was there ever a lot of things I did not know!" He said he would have been very frustrated because of this when he got older. He said I knew that about him and I was the only one he could tolerate to even tell him. He really loved me and respected me as his Mother because I was very patient with him. He depended on me since he was seven.

JS It is great to get all of this insight into his thinking. He was very logical and had a lot of common sense. I knew that he depended on me for support and I always wanted to give it to him. Ryan was a little different but I attributed it to being eccentric because he was so intelligent.

LT He was always asking me questions or telling me how it was, he just knew things. He said, "There is so much society expects you to know and live within these confines and doing everything right. There is so much that is not being taught and I (Mom) needs to go out and do that. Sometimes I felt trapped and forced to fit into a certain confined way of thinking." The irony of his passing is that he had such a smart brain.
Why would God choose something to attack it?

JS I am aware that society certainly expects us to live within confined ways or you become somewhat of a misfit. I do not know exactly what he is referring to that I should be teaching. I guess I will have to wait for further information from Ryan at another time. I am certainly open and willing.

LT He loved compartments in things. I see a backpack.

JS Ryan carried a backpack all through high school, university and even when he was finished school. Ryan compartmentalized his life in so many ways even though he did not structure his life as society expected him to do. He chose to do contract work after he finished university as a software engineer. He was definite that he was not going to work nine to five for a company. I guess he was somewhat of a rebel. He certainly had his own ideas of how he wanted to live.

I thank Laura and others for being my link to Ryan from the Other Side. I have learned a lot about Ryan and how he was thinking both on this earth and from the Other Side. He did not let many people in. He has encouraged me to pass on how I am coping with his loss and I am pleased to do it. I feel by searching for information and a closer connection to Ryan that I have developed a much better appreciation for life itself, a much deeper connection to my Church and God, and a hunger to get to know the members of my family on a much deeper level. He has convinced me that I have something to share and I want to start with my own family and you, if I have something to say that will help deal with your loss.

The List

I decided to create a list of things you could do to help you come back to life after your loss of your loved one. Some you may want to do soon after; others may take weeks or months before you are up to it. There is no right time and no right choice of activity but it is important that you make a move toward doing something as soon as you can. I won't fool you; sometimes you will just be going through the motions like a robot or just pretending behind a mask. It is very difficult! But you should make the effort anyway. I have to say that I realize now that I don't remember much of what happened in the first two years. I have a better recollection of things in the third year.

You should get up each day, get dressed and plan to do something. Occasionally allow yourself a day alone with your thoughts. You will know when that kind of a day comes. I used to say to myself that it was time to get off the merry-go-round. Then, the next day keep motoring. The best way to honour your loved one is to keep on living. I read this so much in the books that I chose and read it in my angel cards often too.

Let's start with the obvious; you need to maintain proper nutrition. Even if you can't eat full meals, then graze all day so you come close to a proper diet.

It is important to get adequate exercise. Even if you don't feel like it, you will feel better even if it is a short walk. Sometimes I would go up and down the stairs during commercials. You can choose to exercise with a friend or do it alone. If you can get back to nature in some ways, it will help to ground you and be less stressed.

Get adequate sleep. If you have trouble getting enough zzzzzzzzzzzzs, then try deep breathing exercises, drink warm milk, have a warm bath or create a routine that allows you to get to sleep.

Talk to your friends or family. You know the ones who will listen. You may be surprised at who all will be available for you after your time of loss. If necessary, find a clergy member or a professional. You could join a bereavement group if that appeals to you.

Laugh. Find a good comedy show or movie on television. It is really good for your heart and your soul to laugh rather than watching the news or violence on TV particularly before going to bed. I found it particularly difficult to watch medical or hospital shows, even to this day.

Use social media (Facebook or Twitter) to see what others are doing who have gone through a loss too. You can also connect with them and "chat" if you wish.

There are many opportunities to volunteer in most communities and they would welcome your assistance. It is difficult to wallow in your own misery when you are focused on helping others. You could volunteer in the local schools, hospitals, seniors' homes or the local food bank to name a few.

You could join a local service club like the Lions, the Rotary Club, or the Civitan Club and others. You will feel good helping the community in which you live. You will meet some new people. I read once that if you help someone your seritonin levels in your brain go up. That's the feel good hormone. The person who receives the help gains seritonin in their brain too. Even if you only witness someone helping another, your serotonin level goes up. Who couldn't benefit from an increase of the happy hormone?

There is an endless list of activities that comes under the heading of hobbies. The really good thing about hobbies is that it puts you in the "zone". That allows you to be fully engrossed in the hobby and not be bothered by your emotions. It is a welcome break. It allows you to forget your grief and worries if only for a little while. Here is a short list of possible activities. I'm sure you have many more that you could add to the list that match your interests: gardening, quilting, knitting or crocheting, sewing, learning to play an instrument, fishing, boating, tinkering with cars, engines, etc. and wood carving.

Play cards. This is something you can do on your own like playing solitaire or play with others on the computer. Perhaps you could join a small group of friends on a regular basis. This gets you out among the land of the living. There may be a club in your area that hosts card games and tournaments. It is a good opportunity to socialize.

Organize your photos. If you are like me most of mine are in shoes boxes just waiting to be organized. This could be part of your healing process. You could create a collage or collection of pictures of your loved one to display in your home. Pictures can also be loaded onto an e-frame. You could create DVDs with photos and give them to other members of the family who would appreciate them. I know that I made books and DVDs at the kiosk at Walmart.

Alternative healing or holistic healing is a subject that Ryan introduced to me as the result of one of my visits to him while he was still able to live in his apartment. But even he knew it was too late for this intervention by this time (or so we thought at the time). He was doing yoga and massage therapy though. These are available in most communities. Ask around for a good one. Word of mouth is a great way to find satisfied customers. Yoga classes are also readily available in a local gym or as a community recreation program. If you don't want to take a class, you can buy a DVD and do it in the comfort and privacy of your own home and in your own time. Deep breathing will likely be part of the yoga experience.

Deep breathing is beneficial to you so often throughout the day. If you are feeling particularly stressed, just do some deep breathing. The best way is to breathe deeply through your nose to the count of four, hold it for the count of four and then exhale through your mouth to the count of four. Do this four or five times throughout the day. You will immediately feel better. The best part is you can do this anywhere.

Along the way, I got interested in Angel Cards after reading a few books about Angels. The cards are a tool to connect you with your angels, spirits or loved ones. This is how the cards work. After clearing the deck of someone else's energy by placing the deck in your non-dominant hand and striking it with your dominant hand, then you shuffle the deck and your energy goes into the deck. Hold the cards to your heart and ask a question or advice for a particular concern. Shuffle the deck to put your energy into the deck and your angels will select the cards to give you some insight or help for your concern. You can select three cards but I like to let them pop out on to the floor. I do them on a daily basis. There are directions at the beginning of the manual that accompanies the deck to describe the various spreads or specific number of cards chosen. It is easy to do yourself for daily guidance; there is no wrong way to do it really. Use your tuition.

I have tried hypnosis. I have read about numerology and tried it. I follow my horoscope daily on the internet. I have tried some aroma therapy especially in my Reiki. Healing with gem stones and crystals intrigued me too. Crystals can also be part of the Reiki treatment to bump up the energy.

There is so much available to use. It simply is a matter of what interests you at any particular time. My focus at the present time is Reiki, Angel cards and writing this book. I am happy that I have chosen the path that I have at the present moment. It has been an integral part of my healing process and I feel that I have been led on this path through my visits to my psychics, my tarot card lady and my Angel Cards. You can believe it or not, but as my sister Mary says, "What ever works".

This list is by no means comprehensive. I am sure you can add so many more things that would be tailored to your need and likes. Hopefully, I have given you a springboard of ideas to start with.

If there has been any good out of losing Ryan to cancer at such a young age, perhaps it is the sharing of my experiences and ideas with you on how to start to cope with your loss too. Perhaps some of my ideas will resonate with you. I have been searching and reading for over three years and maybe I can save you some time. Hopefully I have inspired you in some way to live in the now, keep on living for those who still need you in their lives and all the while remember and honour you loved one. Don't forget the messages from Ryan through the psychics. His message was that THERE IS LIFE AFTER DEATH (AN AFTERLIFE) FOR ALL OF US and we will be joining them sometime in the future.

My Letter to Ryan

Dear Ryan,

I love you very much and I miss you every day. I think of you often throughout each day. So many things remind me of you as you well know. Your smile, your wit, your intelligence and your good looks (wink), are all locked up in my memory. I can recall them in a flash if I need a smile.

Your bedroom will always be your bedroom even though the décor has changed since you left for university. There are many reminders tucked in the closet, such as a couple of shirts that you wore in high school but did not take away to university. Your football jersey with LOWE printed on the back hangs there too. The quilt I made for you when you were first diagnosed with cancer is at the top of the pile of other blankets. The blue plaid flannelette sheets that I bought for you to keep you warm at your Dad's house are there too. The colourful throws that I purchased for your hospital bed to brighten up your room so it would not looks sterile and institutional are used on occasion to keep me warm while watching television in the evening.

I have the crucifix that was on your coffin on my dresser. The picture I took off your Facebook page and framed which lay on your coffin is on my side table beside my chair in the living room. I look at it off throughout the day and greet you in the morning and say goodnight to you each night.

Many other pieces of memorabilia are scattered around our home such as garden stones, hanging dragonflies, a decal on the sliding patio door, candle holders and garden lights. You are ever present in our home and will never be forgotten. As you said to me one day while still in your apartment, "MOM, YOU DON'T HAVE TO BE WITH ME TO BE WITH ME" and I am reminded of what you said each time I see that picture. I truly believe that you are with me each and every day. You said that to me to make me realize that I did not have to travel to be with you so often. That quote meant a lot to me at the time and it means even more to me now that you are gone. I will have that quote engraved on my headstone after I join you in spirit.

I have spent many hours trying to figure out "why" you were taken from us at such a young age. You were only thirty-one; that was exactly half my age at the time. Why could God not haven chosen to take me and allowed you to live a longer life and fuller life? I heard an expression once that God wanted another angel in His garden. I have learned in my reading that you wrote your own chart for your life before you were born and only you would know the answer to that question. When I reach the Other Side, I too, will know that answer. While you were on earth and dying you did not know but now that you are on the Other Side it must be clear to you. As well, you will know if you have accomplished what you came to this earth to accomplish. I have given much thought to this as well. I do not know what your plan was but I do know a lot of things that you have accomplished while on this earth and the appreciation and joy you have shared with others. Your friends' testimonies both at the wake and funeral and on your memorial page are proof to that. I feel I have learned so much about you and your character from your friends. When I join you in Heaven you can share with me your purpose on earth and why you left us so early in the game.

The only thing I can think to do is honour you in some way for the amount of time I have left on this earth. I have decided to learn about ways that I can help others. So far, I have offered Reiki to those who are interested in hands-on healing, by offering Angel therapy through the use of Angel cards and by using the gift of music to bring some enjoyment to seniors. I don't pretend to be an entertainer but I do enjoy leading sing-a-longs with them and joking and interacting with them. I swear that I get as much out of sharing my time with them as they do in the music. I offer these things in your honour because I have learned the therapeutic aspect of doing music through the reading I have done since your passing. You are the one who first inspired me to search for information under the umbrella of holistic or alternative healing. You expressed to me that you wished you had taken part in alternative healing at an earlier stage of your cancer treatments.

I have to let you know that there are many strong memories of you and your brothers growing up and the many ways you lit up my life and made me so very proud of you. I am reminded when I look through the photo albums. You were a very beautiful child with your blonde hair and chocolate brown eyes. I always thought you should have been a child model like some of your friends and acquaintances at Denne Public School in Newmarket. As a student you were exemplary. Good grades came easy to you. You were a great worker and always had your assignments completed before they were due. I never had to bug you to complete your homework or do your assignments. You sure cleaned up in the trophy department at your grade eight graduation. I was so proud! When you entered high school and took band you learned three different instruments and I recall that you told me that you were asked to go to a more senior class to demonstrate your ability to more senior students. Also, you were selected to attend the York Region Band for a week of band experience with others selected from the entire region. I recall being at the final concert with Bob as Director of the board. This was no small feat! What an amazing experience you had!

I am also aware that you were very generous tutoring a number of your friends in high school, particularly in computers. What a generous person you were. In sports, however, that did not come naturally. It was difficult for you to understand why it was so easy for your younger brother, Jon, to excel at sports and you had to really work at it. Jon was a natural at all sports; you had to learn the skills of the game(s). I encouraged both of you to be physically active and if you did not have a physical education class to try out for a team. I recall, the one year you did not have a class and were not on a team that you paid to play hockey. I was pleased that you shared my understanding and importance of being active. Thank you, Ryan for listening. Since you had a car, you were also depended on as being the D.D. (designated driver) in high school and a number of your friends depended on you for that. Again, I was proud of you for that.

In university you studied computers, of course. You were spending most of your waking hours on the computer so I said to you one day that that should be your career because you obviously love working on the computer. I said to all three of our sons that if they were lucky enough to have a job that was their passion it would not seem like you were going to work each day of your adult life. Ryan listened. You started off with computer hardware as your major and I remember the phone call one day near the end of your degree. You said you had some good news and some bad news and which did I want to hear first? I said it didn't really matter since you were going to tell me both anyway. You told me that you wanted to drop hardware and continue with a degree in software. You assured me that you were sure that was what you really wanted. What could I say?

I want you to know that you took a piece of my heart with you when you left this earthly plane and crossed over to the Other Side. I will always miss you. I will honour your existence by serving others in my own way, some of which I am sure I have not fully embraced yet. I still have much to learn but you have certainly given me a goal and perspective for the remainder of my life. I will always remember what you said to me on one of the last days that you lived in your apartment when you were trying to get me to understand that I did not need to visit you on a nearly daily schedule, but I would not listen. I needed to be with you. It took about an hour to drive each way. You said and I quote, "you don't have to be with me to be with me". You also said to save my energy for the end. I replied that I would be there then too. What you said to me was so profound and I take it to heart now that YOU are no longer with me.

I got your message through the psychics that you are alive and well on the Other Side, that there is an afterlife, that you are still around for me, that I can still talk to you and you are listening and that I will meet you again someday when my time comes. You have already shared that you are with my parents and Pappy and you will be there for me when it is my turn to cross over. This information should be comforting for the readers of this book you encouraged me to write and are taking credit for.

Ryan, I will always remember you and love you. Until we meet again, Mom

Let's Talk; let's get the conversation started.

Well, that's my story so far. What about yours? You must have a similar story or you would not be reading this book. You must be searching for answers too. It doesn't matter if your loss is your child, your sibling or your spouse or your friend, you will have many of the thoughts and tribulations that I had and shared with you. You are probably still searching for answers and ways of dealing with your loss. This book is one of the ways I chose to deal with my situation. I started by writing a journal and decided to share knowing others were going through the same thing. I found it very therapeutic. By sharing my thoughts with you, I hope it is helpful and will give you the encouragement to find a way that works for you to go on living.

Personally, I feel it is extremely important to share your grief with family and friends who wish to help you and allow them to express their condolences. Sometimes it is very awkward for both parties at the time but it will get easier. It is very comforting to know that other people care.

I would like to know YOUR story. Perhaps you have some suggestions for me. Everybody deals with grief differently; there is no right way and no wrong way. What works for you today may not be helpful tomorrow. What works for me may not work for you. Feel free to contact me through e-mail, Facebook, twitter or a letter. At the very least, share with someone. It is a good time to think about talking to people you love about illness, dying and death before it happens. Get more comfortable talking about these things that people don't want to talk about until it is necessary. At that point you are so emotional and just plain "numb" that it is very difficult to handle the necessary arrangements. For example, shortly after Ryan passed on, Bob and I discussed what we would want our last wishes to be. We even wrote the words that would be on our headstone. I had already bought a plot in the Catholic cemetery in Almonte, where Ryan is buried, for our final resting place. I also started talking to my sisters and my brother about their arrangements.

Suit yourself, but it is really comforting to know that it has already been discussed and decided. All one has to do is pull out the file and follow through. One of my sisters has already arranged for a prepaid funeral; so has my brother. They feel good knowing that their kids will not be left with that burden.

The Word is all Around You

Many of the topics I have covered are all around you. I have started researching the **Afterlife** and **Heaven** because I wanted to know what really happened to Ryan when he died. That led me to **crossing over** and the **transition**. I started to be interested in **reincarnation.** Have we been on this earth before? I was introduced to the topic of **past lives**. I had been told that I was an old soul and I have lived on this earth many times before, mostly as a woman. I was missing Ryan and I had a very strong desire to communicate with him so I decided to follow up on a suggestion to get an appointment with a **psychic** medium. I have to say it was an extremely uplifting and exciting experience for me and I couldn't get enough. I started to read about **Karma** and **aliens**. Hmmm. That is where this journey really accelerated. I got many of my books at bookstore, used book stores and borrowed some from friends.

Many of these topics are all around us in our sayings, our conversation and the media whether it be through songs, radio, television, DVDs and the silver screen.

Let me share some.

Saying: That's the spirit . . . See you on the other side . . . It was Heaven! . . . What goes around comes around . . . You are as white as a ghost . . . Let me lift your spirit . . . See the light . . . Let your little light shine. You can find many, many more if you just listen.

TV shows: Medium . . . Perception . . . Touched By An Angel . . . Ghost Whisperer . . . I Survived . . . Crossing Over . . . Long Island Medium . . . Saving Hope . . . Third Rock from the Sun . . . Mork and Mindy . . . Rescue Mediums . . . Mentalist . . . Listener . . . Ancient Aliens.

Movies: The Departed . . . Sixth Sense . . . Ghost . . . Poltergeist . . . The Adjustment Bureau . . . Courage . . .

Thank you for listening to my tale of woe. I have learned a great deal on my journey so far and my quest for information to better understand the situation. I know am going to continue seeing my psychics and tarot card lady in the future to continue my link with Ryan. Donna, my Tarot lady, can be put in a trance by her husband and she gets you answers to your questions from her spirit guides. You must have twenty or twenty-five questions prepared for her that you would like answered before the session. I think I will try that. I have no interest in quitting at this point; the quest continues. The one thing I have learned for certain is that there is still a lot to learn about these topics and I have only scratched the surface. My immediate interest is developing my **intuition.** Also, I am looking forward to hearing from you and hopefully we can encourage the world to open up this topic and have the courage to help each other in our deepest hours. Let's get the conversation started.

Light and love,
J.J. Southwell (Judy)

Part Two

Messages For My Journey

Who knew there would be messages for my life for here on out. I was so intent on hearing messages from Ryan that I did not see that he and my spirit guides were giving me further messages for the rest of my life. When I was reading the messages from my tarot card lady and the psychics that I went to, I began to understand that there was another level of information woven in the messages to help me live the rest of my life, at least for the near future. I had been blind to this information until I started organizing the text for this book. So, I started to separate it. I guess I have healed sufficiently to see a little more clearly that much has been given to me in the form of messages from spirit. Perhaps this is a good time to review these messages.

First of all let me tell you that in a reading the message is not always in full sentences, sometimes phrases or words that you try to string together to make sense to you. I have taken the liberty of stringing this information together in a way that makes the most sense to me since it was my reading. You may glean information about the Other Side or Heaven or information that may resonate with your own understanding or beliefs. There was also information given to me for Ryan's brothers, his biological father as well as my husband Bob, but I will not share that with you. It is private in nature and very personal. Because it was MY reading, the information is framed for me. I want to share it with you because it shows the depth of information you can get as well as the encouragement that your loved ones can pass on to you because even though they are gone they still know what is happening to you and want to help you. Let me share with you and tell you it was like receiving an email or text from Heaven from Ryan. I feel like we still have a connection. USING PSYCHICS AND A TAROT CARD READER IS MY LINK.

From JEWEL

J   Who is doing Angel work? Are you doing Reiki? Go within. Focus on what you need to do to strengthen, heal and protect yourself. Try automatic writing. Acknowledge your feelings and express them. Share them or write them in a journal. Always add a dose of humour. You are a healer. You are going to have the hands of a healer. Do chakra opening. Heal with stones and colour. Books will enrich your understanding and power. You will get great rewards.

JJS   I had already purchased my first deck of Angel cards and taken Part 1 of Reiki for my own healing. So I started a journal as an outlet for my feelings. I tried automatic writing with no success to date.

J Pay attention to how situations smell (good or evil). Study aromatherapy. You have great affection and loyalty to others and a respect for the elderly and the sick. Draw upon most ancient wisdom. There will be a change for the better.

JJS I do smell thing when no one else does. At first, I smelled the same as was present when Ryan was dying. It is known as the smell of death. It really is not repulsive, but distinctive. This is an example of where I get ideas of what to read next. I did find aromatherapy and colour therapy very interesting. Remember I took colourful blankets to Ryan at the hospital to brighten the room and his spirits. I already had been volunteering at the Manor in Renfrew which is a home for the elderly. I love to watch the TV show called Ancient Aliens.

From ANGELA

AH Do more writing. You have put it on the back burner. It is experiential. You have a lot to say, including some touching messages. Include female empowerment and no nonsense information. Ryan said, "You are always going to second guess your connection to me, but my Mother will not be deterred." Channel the messages from spirit. It will feel like you are making it up but you are not.

JJS I did continue to write about my experiences, my thoughts and my feelings. I do journal regularly and record my thoughts and feelings. I do not yet channel any messages from spirit but I do look forward to the day that I can. My goal is to be able to communicate to Ryan myself. I will work on this goal until I do.

The rest of the information from Angela was about other people related to Ryan but the information is for their eyes only if they are ever ready to hear it.

From DONNA

DK You are looking for spiritual direction. You are aware and have a lot of knowledge, teaching and counseling skills and you are intuitive. Take up one of the intuitive arts and develop it ie) meditation, healing, or any form of divination such as Angel Cards or gem stones. Reiki is not going to make you rich. You are already starting your new path. It is all about enjoying it, sharing your knowledge. You will see; it will expand.

JJS You must remember that you do not tell these people anything before the reading. She was definitely accurate here. I was already doing meditation, Reiki, and Angel cards.

DK You will get a feeling and the whole story line will follow. You will be using the emotional aspect that the Angel cards will bring out with people and the spiritual connection. Your strength is from the creative side. A lot of people will be coming to you certainly. There has been a big changing pattern in your life and things are starting to open up. You are on the right track for your life. You are searching for answers everywhere and you are getting them from your own instincts and from the research you have been doing perhaps on the spiritual guide level.

JJS   When I do Angel cards with other people I do not seem to have any trouble helping them to understand behind the obvious meaning of the cards and draw out further information. I do notice that a small number of people are definitely interested in my new knowledge. It is encouraging to be told that I am on the right track. I will continue the quest for further information.

DK   You have chosen the 'wishing card' which is a gift from your guides for you specifically. The card was one of the cards from the tarot deck. It is for something that you have always wanted. You can be selfish. Keep it quiet. Just let it go and let it appear. Better yet, write it down, put it under your pillow for three nights and then tuck it away for a while. When you put it in the physical, you are making a contract.

JJS   I did as was suggested. I wrote it, put it under my pillow and then tucked it in a safe place. Now, I am waiting. I am waiting for my wish to come true. You cannot put a time line on it because only on earth is there a timeline as we know it. No one knows my wish. I will reveal it when it comes true. I will shout it out to the world.

DK You have a lot of baggage and a lot of things that you have been dealing with. You have been focusing on family and everybody around you and you haven't taken time to look at yourself. It is time to do something neat for you.

JJS Everybody has baggage. The worst of mine of course is Ryan's illness. It is the worst thing I have ever had to deal with. I always thought that I took time for myself but I guess lately not so much. I'll have to think about that.

DK You may be struggling with a little boredom; that is probably where you are now. That's one of the reasons you are doing so much research.

JJS You must remember that I have told her nothing about the reading and the research that I have been doing. You get a lot of validation along the way when you get a reading.

DK You have been surrounded by children. Children emanate intuitive stuff all the time. They are very intuitive. They just go with the flow. Because you have been surrounded by them, you have absorbed it. Do some further research on intuition. Try astrology or feng shei.

JJS Donna did not know that I was a teacher and Principal of an elementary school for my entire career so of course I was surrounded by children all my life. This is certainly more confirmation that she is accurate in her readings and makes me wants to believe the other stuff about Ryan, spirits and my other deceased relatives.

DK Laughter and humour are very important. It builds energy around you. It is healing.

From LAURA

LT   The spirits are telling you to stop procrastinating. They ask how they are going to help you. You are supposed to be on a stage talking to groups of people. You are supposed to write a book. You are supposed to be a strong empowerment for women. But, right now you have a lack of confidence. It just keeps creeping in. The spirits want to help you speak your truth. Nobody would believe that you actually hand over YOUR power at times. You have much to offer from your intellect and your experiences in your life. You should be sitting there as a psychologist counseling women. You are going to talk about your book. (Well, I guess we are going to see about that.)

JJS   Wow! Yes. They are right. I do procrastinate. I go all out to work on the book, then, I put it on the shelf for a while until the next time I get the urge to continue. I don't know about being on a stage. I would rather be on the sidelines making things happen from there. I will make a concerted effort to finish the book and keep it on the front burner until it is finished. I DO hand over my power at times but I like to think that it is my choice at the time. I think there are very many women that hand over their power to men in particular at times and should stand up for themselves more often. Women have been putting other people first for a long time. At the same time women want to be equal. We have a long way to go yet. I DO want to help women get there. I would enjoy talking to or counseling women. I will look in to that; perhaps in the life coach line. I have done some of this lately informally and I do believe it has been helpful to them.

LT   Have you thought about writing? It is really about your life story and within it is a teaching tool. You should write about dealing with your parents, your first marriage, and the loss of your son. You have a wealth of insight for people. Your book will appeal to a wide demographic because you touch on so many areas ie) the strength of women, losses that women have, the identity that women have in relationships.

JJS   At present my theme is mostly around the loss of Ryan and how I have coped the three years following his passing. I hope in sharing my experience that I can help others in some way.

LT   The spirits are wondering how to get you out of this place of insecurity. They say to just start writing again and don't even worry about how to assemble it; you will have a helper. Because of your education, you are analytical and organized in exactly how things go. Shake it up a little bit. You are not going to be on Parliament Hill, braless, in a red dress! (Who knew spirits had a sense of humour. Maybe it was Ryan; I know he had a great sense of humour). Just move things around and let things flow a bit. They indicate that they know I HAVE been working on it and it is about 80% finished. Well, you just have to do it! They say you do a lot of thinking about it for some time and then you go away and do something else. All you have to do is just say where am I starting because really you are really just letting them channel it, right? They are going to give you a memory. Don't worry about how it is going to fit. Just trust and it is all just going to come together. Somebody will help you put the manuscript together.

JJS   After this reading, I did get back at it and am keeping it on the front burner. I was surprised that they thought that I was 80% finished and it was encouraging to me to complete the book. I thought if I was lucky that I would be about 50% done. Shortly after I was on the internet and found a publisher for my book and paid for it so now I have to finish it. I can back out but it costs me money and I have never left a project incomplete; if I started a project, I was not going to leave it unfinished.

LT   I want to talk to you about your Mother. She was strong enough in her own right, telling you a lot of what NOT to do, but not always telling you what TO do. This is the way she raised you and this is what you learned. With your career of teacher and principal, that solidified it. She was also a bit frustrated in life. She wanted you to be successful in life but she did not know how to help you. She would have liked to have more successes too. She did not teach you that you could succeed and that the sky is the limit. Many women in that generation didn't do that either. She felt a bit trapped but she kept it to herself. She was funny. The spirits tell me this is where this pattern (of insecurity) started for you. You understand that you never wanted to disappoint your

Dad. So, here it is. You have to be successful and nobody ever showed you how to do it.

JJS I have learned a lot about my Mother here. In hindsight it is probably true. She was successful and smart in so many ways. I did not get that she was frustrated. I saw her as a stay at home Mom and housewife and she certainly did that well. Mom and Dad worked very well together to raise our family and never considered that they did anything but their very best. I must add here that my Father DID pass on the idea that I could do anything I wanted to with my life and that I just had to go for it.

LT I think it is your connection to spirit now and trust that you have not gone through all of this to not do a lot more with it. But here is where you hold a bit of your Mother's energy, not a lot of it, and not her frustration but her fear of letting people know how much she knew and how great she really was. She had the feeling that she could do a lot more with her life but she did not want people to think she was unhappy or resentful of her lot in life because that was not true. She wanted both. She could have had a wicked side to her; she would have loved to let loose a little.

JJS Very interesting! I did not realize that I was like my Mom in that manner. I must ponder upon that as a possibility and do something about it.

LT There are lots of red and pink hearts forming in front of me. You have so much to offer other people. Your Mother asks, "How can you keep all of these hearts for yourself?" She is here to help you with your confidence and cheer you on with your success. She wants to be friends and kibitz. She wants to talk about your Dad and how much she loved him but sometimes he got under her skin. She was smiling and winked. Your Father had big energy and it was always about him. Your Mother would say, "For Heaven's sake, when is it about me?"

JJS I never saw my parents argue or fight. They always seemed to get along but I suspect it was because my Mother allowed my Dad to have his way. Don't get me wrong. My Dad was as generous to my mom as we could afford. He was very caring in his own way. I understand how my mother felt with the big energy around.

LT Your Mother asked how you would know when she is around. Well, she loved the clothes hanging on the line, so you are going to smell that smell. Also, she is going to touch your head on the right side and you will twirl your hair and you will think about her and get ideas.

JJS I do get smells fairly regularly and I do not recognize a connection but I will work on figuring that out. I let my hair grow and I do twirl my hair. Now when I twirl my hair I will definitely try to figure out what she might be trying to pass on to me. It could be a new idea or a solution to a problem that I am having.

LT She is telling me she hears you singing. She is around then and she likes that. You give many hearts when you do that.

JJS   Do you remember that I told you that I go out to seniors' homes both in Renfrew and in Lakeland, Florida.

LT   In this reading, Ryan is also encouraging you to go out and tell people about what is not being taught. He says that society expects people to live with certain confinements and do everything right, but there is so much more. He said that I need to do that.

JJS   I certainly need clarification on this statement. I need more information here. Maybe at my next reading I will get more details.

LT   Ryan described our living room as yellow and bright with two large windows and a fireplace. He knows that it is where I do my writing. He prefers to sit in the large deep red chair. It is actually burgundy; that's close enough. He would like to claim ownership of that chair. He sits there from time to time. He said he would like to give me some ideas. He has lots of funny memories.

JJS   Our living room is yellow and bright. There are two large picture windows on opposite walls. One is at the front of the house and the other features the forest out back. I would love some of his ideas. I am not sure these days if my ideas are my own or not. Apparently I am getting some from my Mother and Ryan and my guides from time to time.

I shared these parts of my readings with you to clarify where I got my inspiration to start writing a book and start sharing my thoughts and ideas to you. I had been writing a journal before I started seeing any of my special ladies. Please take any of my ideas and try them. They may appeal to you at different stages of your grief and healing process. The most important message is to live; live in the NOW. That is the present, not the past. The best way to honour your loved one is to go on living your life to the fullness. On the Other Side they worry about us and how we are getting along. You can get a lot of this information watching the psychics from the comfort of your own living room. There are television shows featuring psychics and how they help. I have seen two talk shows in the past week with well-known psychics as special guests who demonstrated their gift. There seems to be a surge of interest in the psychic world these days. If you are still curious then you should seek out one in your area. They are on the internet and you may already know one in your area or someone who has already used their services. I will repeat that I feel that I still have a connection to Ryan each time I go to see a psychic or my tarot card lady. Wouldn't you like to make that connection with your loved one? It is also confirming that there is life in spirit after our life on earth is completed and we will once again meet all our deceased relatives.

Conclusion

Starting as soon as this book is sent to press, I am going to research on developing my intuition further and continue to try to connect to my spirits and guides especially Ryan. I will continue to use the help of my psychics until I am able to get through to Ryan. My personal goal is to be able to "talk" to Ryan myself. When that is achieved I will be ready to write another book and let you know I finally did it. I am convinced that going to see the psychics and the tarot card lady and doing all the reading I have done to date has helped me to accept Ryan's death with some grace and dignity. I have learned that there is an Other Side (Heaven) and it is an amazing place. I have learned that I am going to see Ryan again someday!

Part of **Ryan's legacy** was his mark on the computer world, especially in the Ottawa area with his friends and with the business personnel in various companies. He particularly made an impact on the "ruby on rails" software when he went to Las Vegas to do a presentation.

Ryan was the one who inspired me to check out alternative healing and got me going on researching all of the things that I have read. From there it was my choice to which ones

I would become more knowledgeable about and/or practice. **Ryan's legacy** is also that he wants everyone to know that there is life after death or Heaven which I learned from him through the psychic readings that I experienced. I am the messenger. He was the one to encourage me to write a book and share that with you. He is the one who told me through a medium that we will meet again. He said that he will be there when I die and cross over. I am looking forward to that! Until we meet again Ryan!

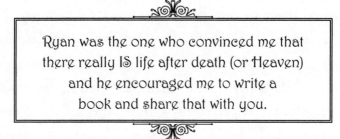

Ryan was the one who convinced me that there really IS life after death (or Heaven) and he encouraged me to write a book and share that with you.

This is Ryan's final resting place. It is graced with a headstone designed and paid for by his older brother, Derek.

Epilogue

Now that you have finished the book, what are you going to do? Hopefully some of the information and suggestions are worthy of you trying them. I truly believe they helped me. Not every day was a good one. But just keep on going and do not be mired in misery. Take the rest of your life and live it to honour him or her in whatever way you decide is right for you. I remind you that I would like to talk to or hear from you if that interests you. I will have an e-mail address available to you, a Facebook page, or you can write me a letter. Find someone close to you that you can talk to; it could be a good family member or a close friend. My girlfriend, Joyce, and I used to say that if everyone had a best friend to tell their troubles to, we would put the psychiatrists out of business and save our money. I would pay her and she would pay me. God bless and good luck on your healing journey.

Light and love,
J.J. Southwell

Favourite Books

Browne, Sylvia *Blessings from the Other Side*
    Life on the Other Side
    Past Lives, Future Healing
    The Other Side and Back Hay House
Choquette, Sonia *Ask Your Guides* Hay House
Dubois, Allison *We Are Their Heaven* Simon & Schuster
Edwards, John *Infinite Quest* Sterling
Montgomery, Ruth *Strangers among Us* Coward, McCann &
    Geoghegan
    Here and Hereafter Fawcett Crest
Peale, Norman *The Power of Positive Thinking* C.R. Gibson Co.
Puryear, Herbert, PhD *The Edward Cayce Primer* Bantam
    Books, Inc.
Van Prague, James *Talking to Heaven*
    Healing Grief
    Unfinished Business Penquin Putman Inc.
Warren, Rick *The Purpose Driven Life* Zondervan
Weiss, Brian, L. *Many Lives, Many Masters* Fireside
Virtue, Doreen *Ask Your Guides* Hay House

I read one hundred and twenty books before writing this book; about twenty of them I read twice because they were so profound and really resonating to me. The ones listed here were some of my favourites.

Acknowlegments

I have a number of people to thank who helped me to survive and helped me on my healing journey since Ryan's passing.

Thank you to all of the authors that provided the books for me to immerse myself in. It was a safe place for me especially in the early days after Ryan's death. I followed a quest for information about death and the afterlife to see if there was any way of knowing that Ryan was okay and could we communicate again someday, somehow.

Thank you to the specialists I sought out to help me get a link to Ryan. Heather is a shamanic practitioner and trained me in Reiki. Laura is a psychic medium and as you have read gave me invaluable information and an amazing link with Ryan and surprisingly to both of my parents, Genny and Tom as well as my maternal Grandmother, Rose. Angela and Jewels supplied me with valuable pieces to the puzzle too. Donna is a tarot card reader and tea leaf reader and was amazingly accurate with information she shared with me. Thank you, ladies.

Various books suggested to me to use angel oracle cards. Some of my ladies used them with their clients too. I found them most helpful and encouraging to use. I still use them daily.

I believe it was synchronicity that led me to Joanne Clark. She is a resident in the park in Florida where we live in the winter months. Joanne was my go-to person when I need help navigating my new computer. She was very knowledgeable and willing to share her expertise with me when needed. I really appreciated the assistance she provided to me.

A very special thank you goes out to my production team at Balboa Press to make my dream of a book become a reality. They were always available to answer my queries whether large or small. They were also patient, flexible and accommodating with my requests to make the book to my liking.

Thank you to my friends and family who will never know how much I counted on them to help me through this dark time. I sought them out on days I just did not want to be alone. I just wanted to "hang" with people that I knew loved me. I would talk about Ryan as if he were still alive. He is still alive in my heart and he always will be.

Thank God for giving me Ryan for an all too brief period. Now I know I WILL see him again when I join him and he will be there waiting for me when I go through the white light because he told me he would be. Thank you Ryan for encouraging me to write this book; it was very helpful in my healing process. Ryan's words were passed on to me through my very special ladies. Now I have shared this information with you. I now know that Ryan is at peace; he is not suffering and he is with other members of my family and his Dad's family. Hopefully you can take this information and apply it to your own grieving process and be more at peace knowing that your loved one is there too.

About the Author

J. J. is a retired elementary school principal. She has a B.A. in psychology and a Master's in Education. With her husband, Bob, she has three sons: Derek, Ryan, and Jon; three stepchildren: Rob, Vicki, and Charlene; and four grandchildren: Kris, Michael, Tanner, and Mackinley and another granddaughter on the way.

Since her son Ryan died of cancer three and a half years ago, she has read 120 books and trained to be a Reiki Master/ teacher to help with her healing journey. She practices with four decks of angel cards daily for her own purposes and will do a reading for anyone who wishes.

J. J. has visited a number of psychic mediums, a shamanic practitioner, and a tarot-card and tea-leaf reader in order to have a link with Ryan. In this book, she would love to share with you the knowledge she gained and messages received from her deceased son.